# geography 360°

Ann Bowen and John Pallister

## Core Book 2

www.heinemann.co.uk
✓ Free online support
✓ Useful weblinks
✓ 24 hour online ordering

**01865 888058**

Heinemann

*Inspiring generations*

Heinemann Educational Publishers
Halley Court, Jordan Hill, Oxford OX2 8EJ
Part of Harcourt Education

Heinemann is the registered trademark of
Harcourt Education Limited

© Harcourt Education Limited, 2005

First published 2005

10 09 08 07 06 05
10 9 8 7 6 5 4 3 2 1

British Library Cataloguing in Publication Data is available
from the British Library on request.

ISBN 0435 35658 5

## Copyright notice

Edited by Caroline Hannan
Designed by hicksdesign and typeset and illustrated by HL Studios
Original illustrations © Harcourt Education Limited, 2005
Printed and bound in Italy by Printer Trento S.r.l.
Cover photo: © Getty Images
Picture research by Beatrice Ray

## Acknowledgements

### Maps and extracts
This product includes mapping data licensed from Ordnance Survey® with the permission of the Controller
of Her Majesty's Stationery Office, © Crown copyright. All rights reserved. Licence no. 100000230.
Page 20 Source B: US Census Bureau. Pages 24, 25 Sources A, D: Home Office. Pages 26, 27
Sources A and B, page 41 Source C: BBC News. Page 49 Sources B and C: World Tourism Organization.
Page 54 Sources A and B, page 55 Sources D, E and F: United Kingdom Tourism Survey. Page 58
Source B: wordtravels.com. Page 67 Source E: Daily Telegraph. Page 140 Source A: Mail on Sunday.
Page 142 Source A: Independent. Page 143 Source C: Guardian.

### Photos
Pages 7, 9, 22, 26, 30, 34, 36, 44, 47, 48, 51, 52, 56, 60, 137: Alamy. Page 117: Cafedirect.
Pages 12, 13, 15, 17, 34, 52, 58, 82, 136: Corbis. Pages 7, 22, 41: Empics. Pages 6, 7, 9,
15, 25, 27, 28, 31, 44, 52, 72, 75, 111, 130, 131, 132, 134, 137: Getty. Pages 5, 32, 128,
129, 135: Harcourt Education. Pages 7, 28, 50, 51: Lonely Planet Images. Page 40: NERC
Satellite Receiving Station. Page 9: Oxford Scientific Films. Pages 5, 9, 15, 32, 128, 129, 135:
Photodisc. Page 138: Reuters. Pages 6, 7: Robert Harding. Page: 119: Roundabout. Page 22:
Syed Jan Sabawoon. Pages 59, 60: Travel Ink. Photographs on all other pages kindly supplied by
author John Pallister.

Every effort has been made to contact copyright holders of material reproduced in this book. Any
omissions will be rectified in subsequent printings if notice is given to the publishers.

**Websites**
On pages where you are
asked to go to
www.heinemann.co.uk/hotlinks
to complete a task or download
information, please insert the
code **6585P** at the website.

# Contents

# >> 1    Introducing Europe

**Can you pick out Europe on this satellite view of part of the world?**

**Where does Europe start and finish?**

## Learning objectives

What are you going to learn about in this chapter?

>    The extent of Europe

>    The political map of Europe

>    The physical geography of Europe

>    The formation of the European Union

# Where is Europe?

> **Understanding where Europe is**
> **Using information in photographs**

Could you draw the boundaries of Europe on to a map? Map **A** shows the continent of Europe. To the west it is bounded by the Atlantic Ocean, to the north by the Arctic Ocean, and to the south by the Mediterranean Sea. It is more difficult to work out the eastern boundary, where Europe meets Asia. This boundary is formed by the Ural Mountains that run from north to south through the Russian Federation, so only part of Russia is in Europe. Turkey is split between Europe and Asia. Turkey's largest city, Istanbul, is in Europe, but most of its land area is in Asia. The North Sea and the English Channel separate the British Isles from mainland Europe.

**A** A political map of Europe

N

16°
ARCTIC
OCEAN

ATLANTIC
OCEAN

Shetland Is.

Orkney Is.

NORWAY

SWEDEN

SCOTLAND

NORTHERN
IRELAND

NORTH
SEA

DENMARK

Go'

Öland

IRELAND

UNITED
KINGDOM

WALES

ENGLAND

NETHERLANDS

BELGIUM

GERMANY

BALT

P

LUXEMBOURG

CZECH
REPUBLIC

42°

14°

FRANCE

SWITZERLAND

AUSTRIA

SLO

HUN

SLOVENIA

ITALY

CROATIA

BOSNI.
HERZEGO

ANDORRA

PORTUGAL

SPAIN

Corsica

Elba

ADRIATIC SEA

BALEARIC IS.

Menorca

Ibiza

Majorca

Sardinia

MEDITERRANEAN

Sicily

8°

MOROCCO

ALGERIA

TUNISIA

MALTA

16°

0°

8°

S E A

# Activities

**1** In a pair or small group, choose *one* of photographs **B–H**. Make sure that every photograph is studied by a group in the class. Note down the key features of the photograph.

a) Where do you think the photograph may have been taken in Europe? Give reasons for your answer.

b) Working with another small group, compare your two photographs and list the similarities and differences. Check that the other group agrees with your description of the photograph.

c) As a class, discuss what you think of when you hear the word *Europe*. Do these images match your ideas of what Europe looks like?

**2** Read the following statements about Europe. Decide which statements are true and which are false.

- Europe is a continent.
- Europe is a group of countries, the largest of which is the Russian Federation.
- The European countries are all next to each other with no sea between them.
- Only part of the Russian Federation is in Europe.
- Part of Europe lies in the southern hemisphere.
- Europe stretches from the Atlantic Ocean in the west to the Ural Mountains in the east.

**3** *Variety in Europe*

a) Write a paragraph to describe the variety of human and physical characteristics in Europe. You can use the work from Activity 1 to help you.

b) If you had a free choice, where in Europe would you prefer to live? Why?

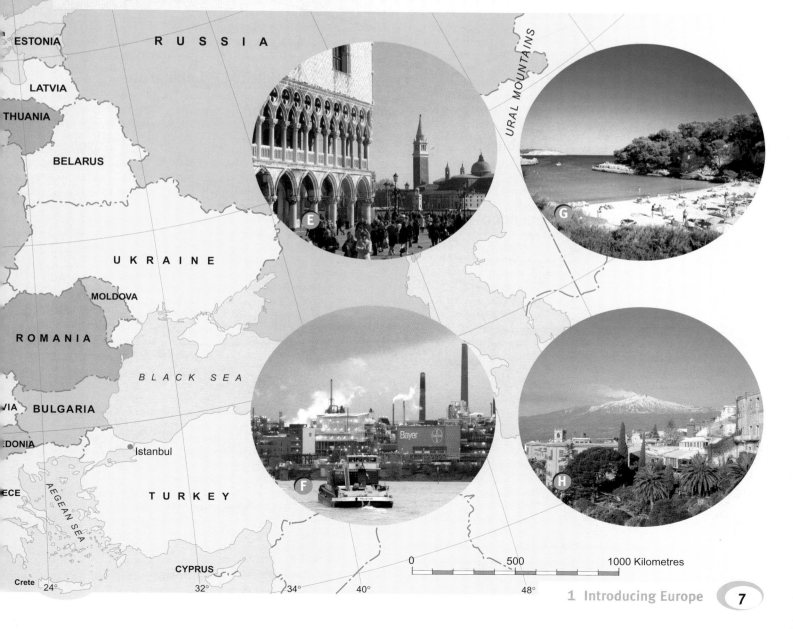

# What does Europe look like?

> Recognising the different landscapes of Europe
> Learning about the major rivers and seas of Europe

Europe is almost triangular in shape and is often called a **peninsula** because it is surrounded on three sides by seas (see map **A**). It also has lots of smaller peninsulas. To the north-west the land is made up of old, hard rocks while the centre of Europe has much younger rocks and many lowland plains. To the south there are ranges of mountains such as the Alps. Some of these high mountains are covered in ice and snow, forming glaciers and ice caps.

**A** The physical geography of Europe

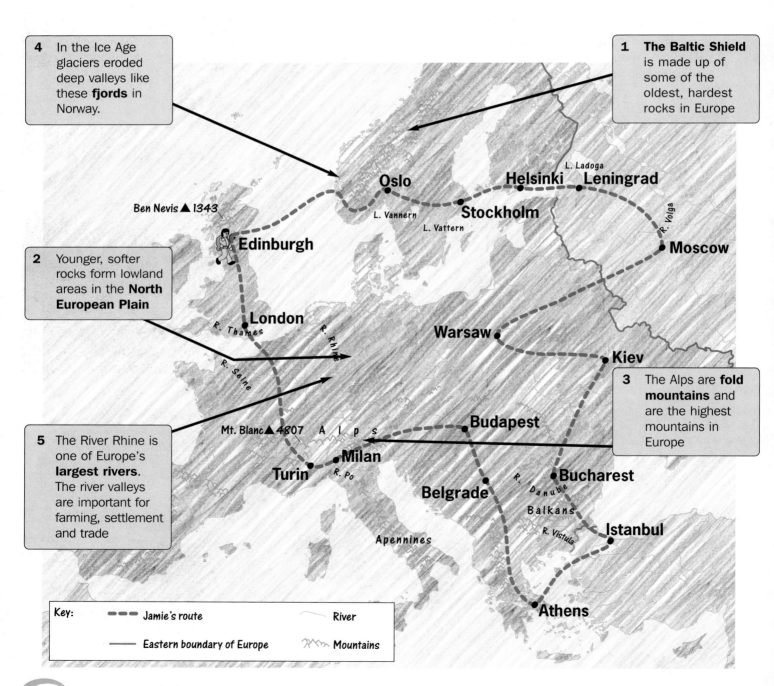

**4** In the Ice Age glaciers eroded deep valleys like these **fjords** in Norway.

**1** **The Baltic Shield** is made up of some of the oldest, hardest rocks in Europe

**2** Younger, softer rocks form lowland areas in the **North European Plain**

**5** The River Rhine is one of Europe's **largest rivers**. The river valleys are important for farming, settlement and trade

**3** The Alps are **fold mountains** and are the highest mountains in Europe

Ben Nevis ▲ 1343

Oslo
L. Ladoga
Helsinki  Leningrad
L. Vannern
Stockholm
L. Vattern
R. Volga
Edinburgh
Moscow

London
R. Thames
R. Rhine
Warsaw
Kiev
R. Seine

Mt. Blanc ▲ 4807  A l p s
Budapest
Milan
Turin  R. Po
Bucharest
Belgrade  R. Danube
Balkans
Apennines  R. Vistula
Istanbul

Athens

Key:
- - - Jamie's route
—— River
—— Eastern boundary of Europe
〰〰 Mountains

## Activities

**1** Make a copy of the table below. Put each of the names below into the correct column – the first one has been done for you.

Alps    Italy    Rhine    Thames    Urals
Iberia (Spain and Portugal)    Pennines    Rhône    Pyrenees
Scandinavia    Danube

| European mountains | European rivers | Peninsulas |
|---|---|---|
| Alps | | |

**2** Choose *one* photograph showing a **landscape** in Europe from this page. Draw a sketch of the photograph (see pages 145–155 of *SKILLS in geography* for more help). Label the physical characteristics on your sketch and add a title.

**3** *Jamie's European holiday*

Jamie lives in Edinburgh and is taking a long holiday after his exams. He hopes to travel in Europe – you can see his planned route on map **A**.

a) Jamie wants to try some activities on his trip. Describe Jamie's route through Europe and match the activities below to the landscapes he will visit:

- Visiting ancient ruins
- Skiing
- Sailing
- Rock climbing
- Cycling in lowland areas.

b) Jamie's friend Bob plans to join Jamie on his trip. Bob wants to visit the famous cities of Paris, Vienna and Venice. Looking at an atlas, plan his route for him.

c) If you had the opportunity to tour Europe describe where you would go and why.

### Key words

**Fold mountains** – mountains formed by rocks being folded and uplifted
**Landscape** – the natural scenery of an area and what it looks like
**Peninsula** – an area of land surrounded on three sides by the sea
**Physical geography** – the natural features on the Earth's surface

# What is the EU?

> Understanding how the European Union was formed
> Practising your map skills

N

**Key**
☐ Members of the EU

0    500    1000 Kilometres

**A** The countries of the EU

## Key words

**EU** – the European Union, many countries in Europe have joined

**Trade** – the selling of goods between countries

**Treaty** – an agreement between different countries

Map **A** shows the countries that belong to the **EU**. Throughout history countries have signed agreements or **treaties** for many reasons. While the Kyoto Treaty (1997) is about protecting the environment, the European Union grew from a trading agreement between the Benelux countries (**Be**lgium, The **Ne**therlands and **Lux**embourg) in 1948.

Source **B** shows a simple history of the development of the European Union. Today the EU has 25 member states, and more want to join. Its influence now goes well beyond that of **trade** into the financial, cultural, environmental and everyday lives of the people of the member states.

| | |
|---|---|
| 1948 | Benelux countries (**Be**lgium, **Ne**therlands and **Lux**embourg) formed an agreement to trade with each other. |
| 1952 | France, West Germany and Italy joined with the Benelux countries to form the ECSC – European Steel and Coal Community. |
| 1957 | These six countries formed the EEC – European Economic Community or 'Common Market' – to co-operate on trade, industry, agriculture and nuclear power. The organisation became known as the European Community or EC. |
| 1973 | The United Kingdom, Denmark and the Republic of Ireland joined the EC, making nine members. |
| 1981 | Greece became the tenth member of the EC. |
| 1986 | Spain and Portugal joined, making twelve members. |
| 1987 | Turkey applied to join but in 2004 is still not a member. |
| 1990 | East Germany reunited with West Germany and became part of the EC. |

| 1993 | The single European market was created. All barriers were supposed to be removed so that people from EC countries could work, study, trade or travel anywhere within the EC. |
|------|---|
| 1995 | Austria, Finland and Sweden joined – fifteen members. |
| 2002 | The launch of the Euro – the single currency adopted by twelve of the member states. |
| 2004 | Ten more countries joined – Cyprus, the Czech Republic, Estonia, Hungary, Latvia, Lithuania, Malta, Poland, Slovakia and Slovenia. |
| 2007 | Bulgaria, Croatia, Macedonia, Romania and Turkey hope to join. |

**B** **A simple history of the EU**

The EU is vast and it needs a huge amount of money to make it work. Member countries pay money to the EU headquarters in Brussels according to how much they can afford. This money is raised from taxes paid on goods. In the UK it is called Value Added Tax or VAT. The EU divides up the money and allocates it into different funds. Source **C** shows where the money went in 2004.

| Agriculture | 42% |
|---|---|
| Regional development and Social Fund | 36% |
| Internal policies, e.g. security, research, transport, energy | 8% |
| External action, e.g. aid to other countries such as Iraq | 8% |
| Administration | 5% |
| Other | 1% |

**C** **How the EU spends its money (2004)**

## Activities

(S) (≣) (A)

**1** Using source **B** and an outline map of Europe, shade in the countries to create a shading map showing the decade in which they joined the EU. Remember to include the islands that belong to each country. (See pages 145–155 of *SKILLS in geography* for more help.)

Use the following key:

☐ 1940–1949    ☐ 1980–1989
☐ 1950–1959    ☐ 1990–1999
☐ 1960–1969    ☐ 2000–2005
☐ 1970–1979

**2** Using your completed map, describe how the EU has expanded. Can you find a pattern?

**3** The main EU buildings are in Strasbourg, Luxembourg and Brussels. Find these cities in an atlas. Why do you think these cities were chosen as the main meeting places?

**4** a) Using *SKILLS in geography*, pages 145–155, draw a pie chart to show the information in source **C**.

b) What is most money spent on?

c) Which fund do you think is used to help areas of high unemployment?

# Living in the EU

> Using GDP to show if some parts of the European Union are more developed than others
> Creating spider diagrams

You might expect that all EU countries would be wealthy. However there can be big differences between them. One way of measuring this difference is to use **GDP** (Gross Domestic Product) (see **A**). Table **A** shows some key characteristics of six European Union countries.

| Country | Population (millions) | GDP per head (US $) | Unemployment (%) | When joined EU |
|---|---|---|---|---|
| Belguim | 10.29 | 29 200 | 7.2 | 1957 |
| France | 60.18 | 26 000 | 9.1 | 1957 |
| Finland | 5.19 | 25 800 | 8.5 | 1995 |
| Portugal | 10.10 | 19 400 | 4.7 | 1986 |
| Poland | 38.62 | 9 700 | 18.1 | 2004 |
| UK | 60.09 | 25 500 | 5.2 | 1973 |

**A** Key characteristics of six EU countries, 2002–3

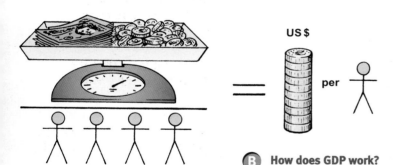

US $

= per

**B** How does GDP work?

GDP is a measure of the wealth of the country. It is worked out by dividing the total of the money a country gains from the production of goods and services by its population (see **B**).

Differences in wealth can also lead to differences in opinion – see source **C**.

## YOUR VOICE: EU ENLARGEMENT

# Marcin Jasinski, 18, Warsaw, Poland

I feel disappointed that we will not have complete equality with earlier members

Although I am glad that Poland can join the EU, I feel disappointed that we will not have complete equality with earlier members.

We have many skilled workers with much to contribute who do not have jobs because unemployment is high. Of the EU countries, Poles will only be allowed to work in the UK and Ireland. This seems unfair.

# João Rodrigues Lopes, 28, Lisbon, Portugal

**I believe that European expansion is a good thing**

The benefits of joining the EU seem obvious to me. Although not everyone agrees, I believe that European expansion is a good thing. It will be a step forward to unite Europe as a single democratic body.

# Anna Naudi, 78, Mosta, Malta

**I think that belonging to the EU will be a blessing**

I am pleased to see Europe being enlarged to include Malta and other countries. After living through Nazi occupation and the threat of communism, I think that belonging to the EU will be a blessing.

**C** Three views on the expansion of the EU

## Activities

(S) (📄) (A)

1  a) Using the worksheet from your teacher, complete a table like the one below to rank the countries according to the percentage (%) unemployment.

| Rank | Country according to unemployment (smallest first) |
|------|-----------------------------------------------------|
| 1 | Netherlands |
| 2 | Cyprus (GC) |
| 3 | Sweden |
| | |

   b) In your list colour the countries that joined the EU in 2004.

2  a) On an outline map of Europe, draw a choropleth or shading map (see pages 145–155 of *SKILLS in geography* for more help) to show the GDP of countries. Use the following key:

   0–9999        20 000–29 999

   10 000–19 999     30 000 and over

   b) On the map underline the names of those countries that joined the EU in 2004.

   c) Discuss in pairs or small groups what you think the advantages and disadvantages of the enlargement of the EU will be. Share *at least one* of your advantages and disadvantages with the rest of the class. As a whole class create two spider diagrams to show your opinions.

### Key word

**GDP (Gross domestic product)** – the amount of money a country makes from the production of goods and services divided by the total population; the higher the GDP, the richer the country

### SKILLS

**How to draw a spider diagram**

1 Draw a circle (the 'body') in the middle of your page. Write the title in it, e.g. 'Advantages of the EU'.
2 Draw lines ('legs') away from the circle.
3 Write an advantage at the end of each line.
4 You could draw a small sketch beside each advantage.

*For more help* see page 155 of *SKILLS in geography*.

# Investigation – what are the advantages and disadvantages of Country X's membership of the EU?

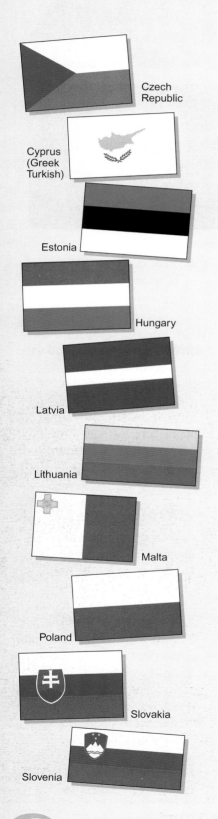

Czech Republic

Cyprus (Greek Turkish)

Estonia

Hungary

Latvia

Lithuania

Malta

Poland

Slovakia

Slovenia

You are going to investigate one of the countries that joined the EU in 2004.

First choose your country and check your choice with your teacher.

You should not produce more than four sides of A4. You could use ICT – a word-processing or presentation software package – to present your work. Remember to include maps, diagrams, photographs and graphs. Make sure that you include the stages in Box **A**.

To help you, take a look at the websites about Europe on the Hotlinks site (see page 2).

Use the mark scheme from your teacher to help you assess your work.

---

It is important to set out your work clearly. You should include a *beginning, a middle* and *an end*.

**1 A beginning**

- A front cover – the title, a picture or map, your name and class.
- A contents list – of all headings in the work.
- An introduction – what is your investigation about, which country are you studying and why did you choose it?

**2 A middle**

Here describe the characteristics of your country. Use the checklist below to make sure that you have included information about the following themes:

- The physical geography of the country – mountains, lowlands, deserts, natural vegetation, rivers, lakes and seas, the climate, etc. A map would be a good idea here.
- Any natural hazards, e.g. earthquakes, volcanoes, floods, drought.
- The human geography – population, cities, culture, religion and economy (agriculture, industry, tourism, etc.)
- What advantages will the country bring to the EU?
- What does the country hope to gain from membership of the EU?

**3 An end**

Write a conclusion to summarise the advantages of the country's membership of the EU for the country and the EU as a whole.
And finally...

Always include a bibliography – this is a list of books, websites and other information used to produce your investigation.

 **Organising your investigation**

# >> 2    Who are the Europeans?

On the world scale Europe has a high population, but not everywhere is settled. Study these photographs. Can you suggest why there are lots of people in some places and not very many in others?

## Learning objectives

What are you going to learn about in this chapter?

> The population distribution and density in Europe
> How Europe's population has changed over time
> The population structure of Europe
> Migration and asylum-seekers in Europe
> The similarities and differences between the UK and Poland

High density population: Paris, France

Low density population: Uig, Scotland

# Where do people live in Europe?

> Understanding why some places have lots of people and some have very few
> Learning how to measure populations

## How to work out population density

**Population density** is the number of people living in a country per square kilometre. You can work out this out by using the formula:

$$\text{Population density} = \frac{\text{Number of people in the country}}{\text{Country's total area (km}^2\text{)}}$$

For example: 58 million people live in France, and the area is 544 000 km², so the population density is 106 people per square kilometre.

The **distribution** of **population** is the way people are spread across a landscape, while the density shows how many people live in an area. Source **A** shows the difference between density and distribution.

On the world scale Europe is densely populated. Europe, south-east Asia and the north-east of North America are among the world's most densely populated regions (**B**). However, within Europe the distribution of the population is very uneven, with areas of low, medium and high density of population (**C**).

**A** Population distribution and density

### Each area is 1km²

**1**

Density = $\frac{1 \text{ person}}{1 \text{km}^2}$ = 1 person/km²

**2**

Density = $\frac{4 \text{ person}}{1 \text{km}^2}$ = 4/km²

**3**

Density = $\frac{4 \text{ person}}{1 \text{km}^2}$ = 4/km²

**4**

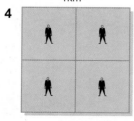

Density = $\frac{4 \text{ person}}{4 \text{ km}^2}$ = 1/km²

The population densities in 1 and 4 are the same, 1/km², although the area is larger in 4.

The population densities in 2 and 3 are the same, 4/km², but notice how the distribution is different. In 2, people are clustered together but in 3 they are more spread out.

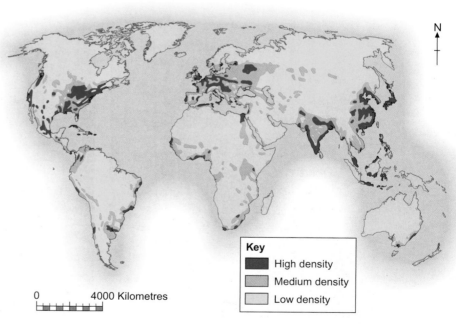

N

Key
- High density
- Medium density
- Low density

0    4000 Kilometres

**B** Where people live worldwide

On map **C** a **core region** can be recognised where population densities are very high. This area has many advantages for the settlement of people such as flat, fertile land, a reliable water supply, a reasonable climate and raw materials. This zone of very high density of population is sometimes called the Manchester–Milan axis because it stretches from Manchester in the UK to Milan in Italy. The axis contains some very large, densely populated cities (photo **D**).

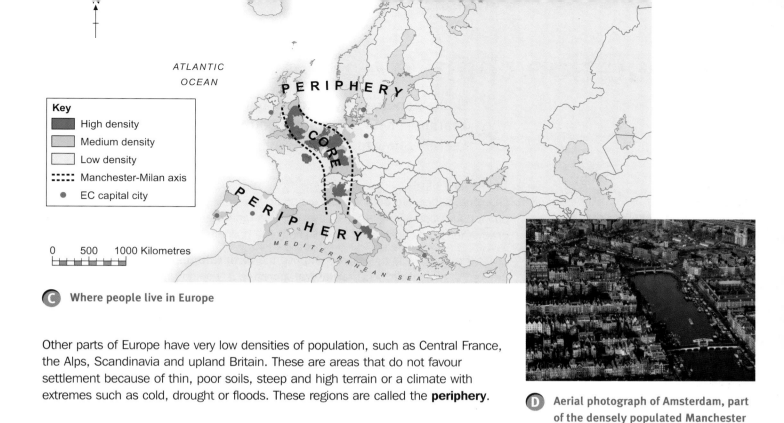

ATLANTIC OCEAN

PERIPHERY

CORE

PERIPHERY

MEDITERRANEAN SEA

**C** Where people live in Europe

Other parts of Europe have very low densities of population, such as Central France, the Alps, Scandinavia and upland Britain. These are areas that do not favour settlement because of thin, poor soils, steep and high terrain or a climate with extremes such as cold, drought or floods. These regions are called the **periphery**.

**D** Aerial photograph of Amsterdam, part of the densely populated Manchester –Milan axis

## Activities

**1** Find the area where you live on map **C**.

　a) What type of population density does your local area have?

　b) Is your area part of the core or periphery in Europe? Give reasons for your answer.

**2** In this activity you are going to complete a choropleth or shading map of Europe. (See pages 145–155 of *SKILLS in geography* for more help.)

　a) Look at the Worksheet table that your teacher will give you. Complete the table to show the densities of population for the European countries.

　b) Choose *one* colour to complete your key for the map: light shading for densities below 100 people per km$^2$; medium shading for densities between 101 and 200 people per km$^2$, and heavy shading for those with densities over 201. Then use the shades chosen to colour in an outline map of Europe according to the data in the table.

　c) Can you recognise the core and periphery? Compare your map with map **C** – which one does the better job? Why?

　d) Try to suggest why the population density for a whole country may be misleading.

**3** Study this list of factors affecting population density. Copy them into a table like the one below to show which ones would encourage a high density of population and which would encourage a low density of population.

- A moderate climate with no extremes
- Thin, rocky soils
- High steep land where tractors cannot be used
- Gently sloping land – easy to build transport routes
- Gently sloping land that is easy to farm with fertile soil
- Areas of drought where it is difficult to farm
- High land covered in snow and ice for more than half the year
- Nearby rivers provide a reliable water supply

| High density of population | Low density of population |
|---|---|
| A moderate climate with no extremes | |

**4** Think about your own local area. Which of the factors above apply to it? Complete a paragraph that starts:

*My local area has a _____ population density because it has...*

# Population change – it's a numbers game

> Understanding why Europe's population has grown over time
> Learning about birth rates, death rates and natural increase
> Learning how to draw a living graph

## Key words

**Birth rate** – the number of births per 1000 people per year

**Death rate** – the number of deaths per 1000 people per year

**Migration** – the movement of people

**Natural decrease** – when death rate is greater than birth rate

**Natural increase** – when birth rate is greater than death rate; birth rate minus death rate is the growth rate of the population

The number of people who live in your street or village or town is constantly changing: babies are born, people die and people move in and out. Information about population is used to decide how much money an area might get from the EU or whether a new hospital or school should be built, so it's important to get it right.

To work out population, geographers use the **birth rate**, **death rate** and the amount of **migration** (**A**). The **natural increase** is worked out by subtracting the death rate from the birth rate. Most countries in Europe, including France and Ireland, have a natural increase in population – this means that the population is growing. In other countries, such as Germany and Romania, more people are dying than are being born so there is a **natural decrease** in population. Figures **B** and **C** show how and why the population has changed in Europe.

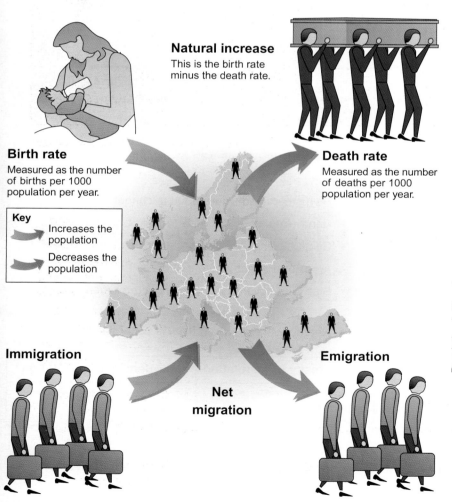

**Natural increase**
This is the birth rate minus the death rate.

**Birth rate**
Measured as the number of births per 1000 population per year.

**Death rate**
Measured as the number of deaths per 1000 population per year.

**Key**
→ Increases the population
→ Decreases the population

**Immigration**

**Net migration**

**Emigration**

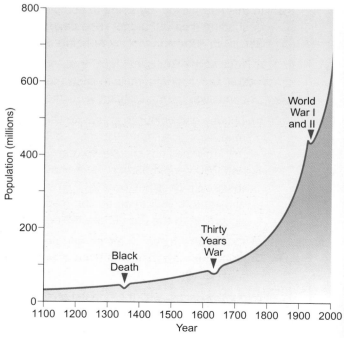

**B** Population change in Europe

**A** Factors causing population change in Europe

The population grew very slowly up until about 1750. At this time both birth rates and death rates were high.

From 1750 to 1950 the population began to grow more quickly as medical care and water supplies began to improve.

In the late 20th century population stabilised. But in some European countries the populations have begun to decrease. When birth rates have fallen below death rates, we say that the population is below replacement level. These countries are worried about this and some are now encouraging higher birth rates so that the population begins to grow again. People are also living longer so the population is ageing – there are fewer young people and more older people.

**C** shows some of the reasons why birth and death rates have fallen.

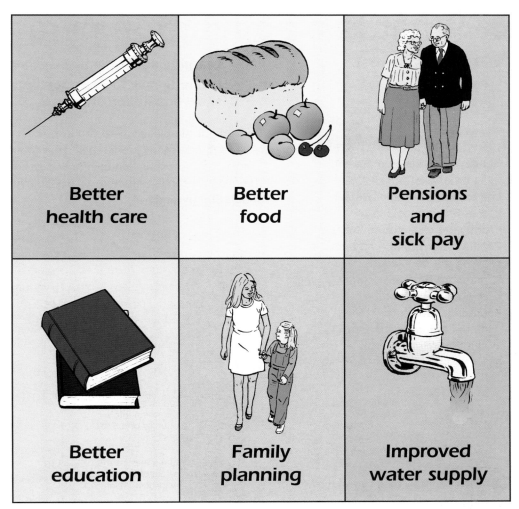

| | | |
|---|---|---|
| **Better health care** | **Better food** | **Pensions and sick pay** |
| **Better education** | **Family planning** | **Improved water supply** |

**C** Why did the population in Europe change?

## Activities

**1  How the population in Europe has grown**

Make a copy of the graph in **B** and convert it into a living graph by adding these labels in the correct places:

- 1750  The Industrial Revolution begins
- 1800  Death rates start to fall
- 1600  Birth rates and death rates high
- 1950  Birth rates falling
- 2000  Birth rates and death rates are low.

**2**  a) Describe the shape of your living graph.

b) How do you think the graph will look by 2500? Explain your answer.

c) When was Europe's population growing very slowly? When was it growing very quickly?

d) Try to suggest reasons why Europe's population growth has changed over time.

### SKILLS

**How to draw a living graph**

1 Draw your graph outline and label the axes. Put the years along the bottom and the population up the side.
2 Plot the graph to show how the population has changed over time.
3 Add the labels in the correct places on the graph.
4 Add a title to your graph.

*For more help* see page 151 of *SKILLS in geography*

# What is a population pyramid?

> Learning about the age–sex structure of populations
> Learning how to draw population pyramids and how they show population structure

## Key words

**Gender** – the sex of a person, male or female
**Life expectancy** – the average age to which people in a country are expected to live
**Population pyramid** – a graph showing the population structure of an area, country or region
**Population structure** – the numbers of males and females in different age groups in a population

Think about the place where you live. How many people in the local area are male, and how many are female? How many are young people, adults or elderly? Dividing up the population by age and **gender** shows the **population structure**. The age and gender structure of a population can be shown by drawing a **population pyramid** (**A**).

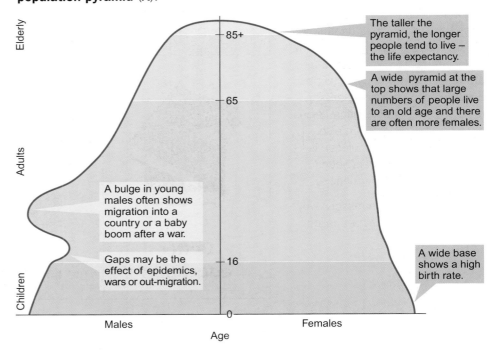

The taller the pyramid, the longer people tend to live – the life expectancy.

A wide pyramid at the top shows that large numbers of people live to an old age and there are often more females.

A bulge in young males often shows migration into a country or a baby boom after a war.

Gaps may be the effect of epidemics, wars or out-migration.

A wide base shows a high birth rate.

**A** What is a population pyramid?

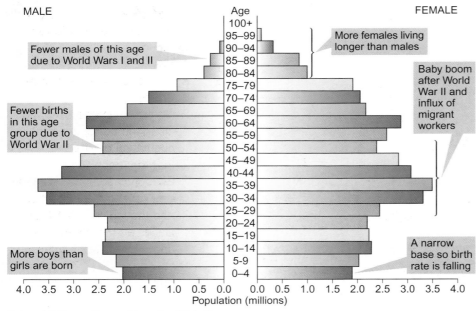

Fewer males of this age due to World Wars I and II

More females living longer than males

Baby boom after World War II and influx of migrant workers

Fewer births in this age group due to World War II

More boys than girls are born

A narrow base so birth rate is falling

*Source: US Census Bureau, International Data Base*

**B** Population pyramid for Germany, 2002

Different places have different population pyramids. A place's population pyramid may also change over time. A population pyramid can tell us about the population history of a country. Look at the pyramid for Germany in **B**.

Some pyramids show that more boys than girls are born. However, more boys die in infancy, so the numbers usually even out in the younger age groups. Females have a longer **life expectancy**, that is, they tend to live longer, so population pyramids often show larger numbers of elderly females. In many European countries there are gaps on the male side because so many men died in the World Wars. You can see population pyramids with different shapes in **C**.

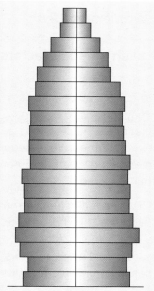

(i) A pyramid may have a narrow base if the birth rate is less than the death rate. Births may have fallen due to improved birth control or women staying in education and having a career. This is happening in some European countries.

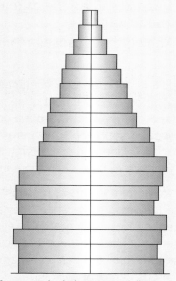

(ii) There may be bulges, especially among young adults in countries where there is high immigration. These may be because young males have moved into the country looking for work and a higher standard of living.

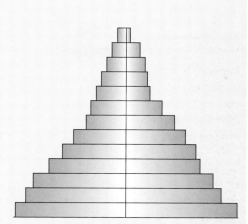

(iii) In some pyramids the shape may be triangular. This indicates that there are high birth and death rates. This is usually in less developed regions.

**C** The different shapes of population pyramids

## Activities

**1** a) Use the information in **D** to draw a population pyramid for the UK in 2000.

   b) Add these labels in the best places:
   - More young males than females
   - More elderly females than males
   - Gap in males     • Narrow base

   b) Suggest reasons to explain each of the labels.

**2** Go to the Hotlinks site (see page 2) to find the Census data for 2001 on the Internet.

   a) Find the age–sex structure for your local area. You could choose your town, ward or county.

   b) Draw a population pyramid for the data.

   c) What are the similarities and differences between your pyramid and the one for the UK as a whole? Suggest reasons to explain the differences.

**3** Go to the Hotlinks site to find population pyramids for countries around the world.

   a) Choose *one* country and study the pyramids for 2000, 2025 and 2050. Label the pyramids to show their key characteristics and suggest reasons for the changes shown.

   b) What do you think the pyramid will look like in 3000? Give reasons. Draw a sketch of the pyramid and label it.

| Age | Males | Females |
|-----|-------|---------|
| 0–14 | 9.6 | 9.2 |
| 15–29 | 9.4 | 9.4 |
| 30–44 | 11.1 | 11.5 |
| 45–59 | 9.4 | 9.5 |
| 60–74 | 6.3 | 7.0 |
| 75–89 | 2.6 | 4.3 |
| 90+ | 0.2 | 0.5 |

**D** Population (in millions) for the UK, 2000

### SKILLS

**How to draw a population pyramid**

1 Show the male population on the left and the female on the right.
2 Draw a horizontal axis with 0 in the middle. The scale can be in either percentages or numbers.
3 Draw a vertical axis from the 0. Divide into age groups, e.g. 0–4, 5–9, 10–14, etc.
4 Draw bars horizontally for each age group and gender.
5 Label the axes and add a title.

*For more help* see page 150 of *SKILLS in geography*

# People on the move

> Understanding the differences between emigration and immigration
> Knowing the causes of migration – push and pull factors

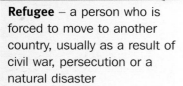

**Key word**

**Refugee** – a person who is forced to move to another country, usually as a result of civil war, persecution or a natural disaster

The population of regions or countries can change quite dramatically as a result of migration or the movement of people. People may move into a country (immigration) or move away from a country (emigration). Migration may be *international*, when people move from one country to another. When people move from place to place within a country it is called *internal migration*. In Europe in recent years there have been more immigrants than emigrants.

People move for a variety of reasons. Sometimes factors make people move because they do not like where they are living. These are called *push factors* because they 'push' the person away from where they live. Other people move because factors attract them to a new place. These are called *pull factors* because they 'pull' the person towards the new destination. Table **A** shows a variety of push and pull factors.

In some cases people are forced to move (see photo **B**). **Refugees** are people forced to move out of their area or country because of push factors such as famine, civil war or political oppression. Migration can therefore be *voluntary* or *forced*.

| Push factors | Pull factors |
|---|---|
| • Unfavourable climate | • Well paid jobs |
| • Lack of services | • Entertainment |
| • Natural disasters, e.g. famine, earthquake, flood | • Education |
| • Civil war | • Moving to be with relatives |
| • Government attitudes | • Higher standard of living |
| | • Health care and welfare benefits |

**A** Reasons for migration

**B** Afghan refugees outside United Nations camp in Kabul, Afghanistan

**C** Where is this family moving to – around the corner or abroad? Why are they moving?

Map **D** shows some historical migrations. Some people migrated from poor to rich countries, some to escape war. Some moved because of their religious beliefs. Some were taken and sold against their will. Migrations happen all the time. In 2004, people from Sudan in Africa were forced to move out of their homes, while British people continued to leave for the sunshine in Australia and Spain.

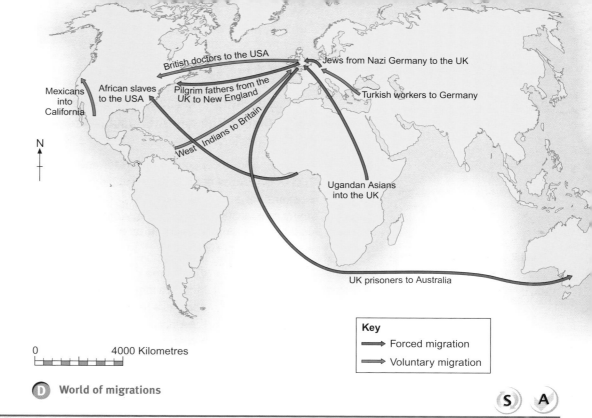

British doctors to the USA
Jews from Nazi Germany to the UK
Mexicans into California
African slaves to the USA
Pilgrim fathers from the UK to New England
Turkish workers to Germany
West Indians to Britain
Ugandan Asians into the UK
UK prisoners to Australia

N

0          4000 Kilometres

| Key | |
|---|---|
| ⟹ | Forced migration |
| ⟹ | Voluntary migration |

**D** World of migrations

## Activities

(S) (A)

**1** Look at photo **C**. Have you or your family ever moved? How far did you move? Why did you move?

a) Produce a class survey of everyone's answers.

b) Can you spot any patterns? For example, do most people move short or long distances?

c) What are the main reasons why people have moved?

**2** *Tops and tails*

Match each word with the correct definition.

| Word | Definition |
|---|---|
| Immigration | Something that attracts people to a place |
| Push factor | People moving out of a country |
| Migration | People moving into a country |
| Pull factor | The movement of people |
| Emigration | Something that makes people move away from a place |

**3** Study source **A**. Rearrange the push and pull factors into a copy of the table below.

| Likely to lead to forced migration | Likely to lead to voluntary migration |
|---|---|
| | |

**4** Choose one of the migrations marked on map **D**.

a) Research the migration by using the Hotlinks site (see page 2). Create a fact file that includes the following information:

- When did the migration take place?
- How many people were involved?
- Where did they emigrate from?
- Where did they migrate to?
- Why did they migrate?
- What were the advantages and disadvantages for the migrant?
- Suggest any advantages and disadvantages for the countries the migrant moved from and moved into.

b) Swap your fact file with a partner. Say what you liked about theirs and suggest how it could be improved.

- Have they included all the information that was asked for?
- Is it clear where the migrants came from and to?
- How clear are the reasons for the migration?
- Have they described the advantages and disadvantages to the migrant of the movement?
- What have the losing and receiving countries gained or lost?

# Asylum-seekers in Europe

> Learning about asylum-seekers – facts and figures
> Discussing whether asylum-seekers should be allowed to stay

In 2002, 430 000 people applied for asylum in Europe (see graph **A**). Over 103 000 (25 per cent) of these applied for asylum in the UK. Many **asylum-seekers** are attracted to the UK because they speak some English and because many nationalities live here. They may also believe that western European countries are democratic and prosperous.

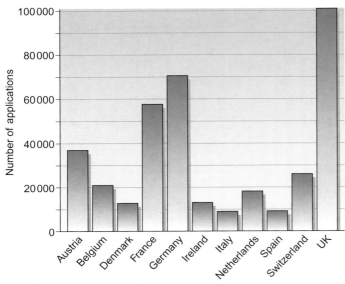

Source: © Crown copyright. Published by the Home Office

**A** Applications for asylum in Europe, 2002

Most people applying for asylum live in fear of their lives in their home countries because of wars and political oppression. Most asylum-seekers are male, under 30 years old and come from Asia, Africa or the Middle East. Many asylum-seekers to the UK come from Iraq and Afghanistan, countries affected by wars, or Zimbabwe, where there is political repression. Most of those hoping to migrate into Europe feel that they have no choice. If they remain in their home country they will be killed.

In 2002 about 75 per cent of asylum-seekers to the UK were allowed to stay. Some were provided with accommodation by a Government agency, with Glasgow (5665), Birmingham (3555) and Liverpool (1925) playing host to the most people.

Look at source **B**. People hold different views about asylum-seekers. Some people are against Europe and the UK accepting them, while others argue for their integration into Europe.

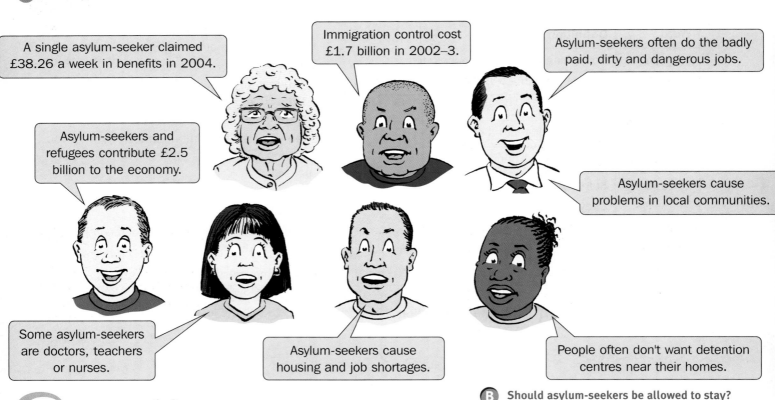

A single asylum-seeker claimed £38.26 a week in benefits in 2004.

Immigration control cost £1.7 billion in 2002–3.

Asylum-seekers often do the badly paid, dirty and dangerous jobs.

Asylum-seekers and refugees contribute £2.5 billion to the economy.

Asylum-seekers cause problems in local communities.

Some asylum-seekers are doctors, teachers or nurses.

Asylum-seekers cause housing and job shortages.

People often don't want detention centres near their homes.

**B** Should asylum-seekers be allowed to stay?

## Activities

**1** Study graph **A**.

a) Which *three* countries received the most applications from asylum-seekers?

b) Suggest some reasons why these countries were popular.

c) For what other reasons do asylum-seekers want to migrate?

**2** Draw a pie graph to show the information in source **D**. (See pages 145–155 of *SKILLS in geography* for more help.)

a) Where do most asylum-seekers come from?

b) Why do you think there are so many asylum-seekers from Europe?

**3** Study the pie graph in **E**.

a) What percentage of asylum-seekers are under 30 years old?

b) Why do you think most asylum-seekers are male and under 30?

**C** Asylum-seekers try to find a way through the Channel Tunnel

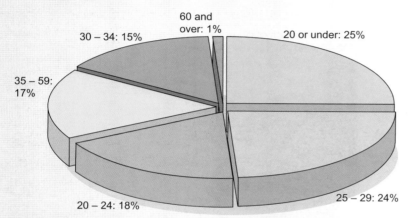

**E** Asylum-seekers in the UK by age group, 2002

- 20 or under: 25%
- 25 – 29: 24%
- 20 – 24: 18%
- 35 – 59: 17%
- 30 – 34: 15%
- 60 and over: 1%

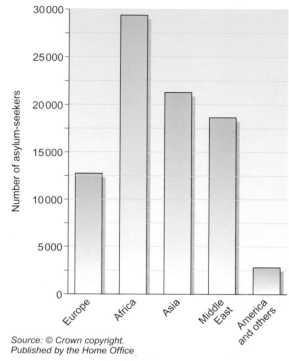

Source: © Crown copyright. Published by the Home Office

**D** Where asylum-seekers to the UK came from, 2002

**4** **What are your views about asylum-seekers?**

Hold a class discussion about whether asylum-seekers should be allowed to stay. Work in small groups; each group should take on one of the roles below.

- An asylum-seeker – choose your country, making up a name if you like.
- The government of the UK.
- The government of the asylum-seeker's country.
- The asylum-seeker's family left behind.
- The immigration authority.
- A UK taxpayer.
- A member of the British National Party (BNP), who oppose immigration.
- A charity that supports asylum-seekers.
- A local resident where a detention unit is planned.

Research information about asylum using the Hotlinks site (see page 2) and write a short presentation to represent your case.

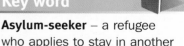

**Key word**

**Asylum-seeker** – a refugee who applies to stay in another country because they face persecution and possibly death in their home country

# Feelings running high!

> Finding out what it is like to be an asylum-seeker
> Exploring the difference between asylum-seekers and economic migrants

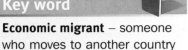

**Key word**

**Economic migrant** – someone who moves to another country for a better standard of living

Asylum-seekers leave their home country because they face persecution or even death. **Economic migrants** hope to find work and a better quality of life in another country – these migrants are not usually welcome in the UK. The big problem for the authorities is judging whether people are genuine asylum-seekers or economic migrants.

On pages 24–25 you discussed whether asylum-seekers should be allowed to stay in the UK. What are your feelings about asylum-seekers? Sources **A** and **B** show some real-life experiences of asylum-seekers in the UK.

# I had to leave my children behind

**As a report says too little is being done to help integrate refugee women into British society, BBC News Online looks at the experience of a Somali woman trying to rebuild her life in the UK.**

Selima, 27, has not seen her two young sons for three years.

She was forced to leave her home in Somalia because her family belonged to a minority ethnic group. They were being persecuted by a dominant tribe in the country's civil war.

Her father was taken away and murdered, and she had to watch her aunt being raped in the family home.

Her husband was imprisoned before managing to escape and flee to Ethiopia.

Selima initially remained in Somalia where she lived in fear of being raped.

"My mum told me I had to escape because I was a young woman," she said.

"She said it was better for her to die than for me."

"I got very depressed and tried to kill myself" Selima

One day in 1999, fierce fighting broke out in Selima's town, and her people scattered.

"Everyone panicked and I was separated from my family," she said.

"I fled to… Ethiopia, where I stayed with my uncle."

"He found the money to get me to the UK."

After arriving, Selima lived in London for two years, but found it extremely hard to adjust – especially without her children.

"Everything was totally different," she said.

## Support network

"I had to ask people to help me do everything, and I spoke very little English so I needed an interpreter to help me.

"It was like being dropped in the ocean and I couldn't bear to live without my children."

Selima consulted her doctor who referred her to a psychologist to help her overcome her depression.

She also found support from a network of Somali friends in Southampton.

She attended college and soon developed excellent English.

She began volunteering as an interpreter with the Refugee Action charity, and through that work found her present job as a bilingual assistant helping Somali schoolchildren.

## My dream

She loves her work, but still misses her children – now aged four and six – terribly.

In July, she was told she would be granted refugee status.

She recently managed to contact her mother through a family tracing service and learned that her children are safe and well.

"My dream is that one day soon I will be reunited with my children."

"There are so many women like me out there" Selima said.

*Friday, 21 February 2003*

 **Selima's story. Reproduced from BBC News at bbcnews.co.uk**

## ASYLUM POLICY SPARKS HIV CONCERN

Doctors are concerned that the UK policy of dispersing asylum-seekers may lead to increased HIV transmission.

## MENTOR SCHEME FOR YOUNG REFUGEES

A scheme to help young asylum-seekers in Liverpool to adjust to life in the UK is launched.

## JAILING ASYLUM-SEEKERS 'MUST END'

The United Nations' agency for refugees protests over the detention of asylum-seekers in the UK's prisons.

## Asylum centre appeal date delayed

Protesters may have to wait another two months for Court of Appeal decision on a new asylum centre.

**B** UK headlines from news stories about asylum-seekers, 2004. Reproduced from BBC News at bbcnews.co.uk

**C** Somali asylum-seeker in Islamabad, Pakistan

## Activities

1   Read carefully about the experiences of the asylum-seeker in **A**. Use what you have read to contribute to a class discussion about:

  •   the push factors that force people to move to the UK

  •   the pull factors that attract people to come to the UK

  •   the advantages of migration to the asylum-seekers

  •   the disadvantages of migration to the asylum-seekers

  •   the response of the government, the media and the general public to asylum-seekers

  •   your own response to asylum-seekers.

2   Imagine you are a young asylum-seeker who has moved recently into your local area. Write about your experiences. You should answer these questions in your writing:

  •   Why were you forced to leave your home country?

  •   Why did you come to the UK?

  •   Who did you have to leave behind?

  •   What has been your experience of living in the UK?

  •   What are your feelings and hopes for the future?

# Poland – a new entrant to the EU

> Finding out the key facts about Poland's population
> Understanding the similarities and differences between the population in Poland and the UK

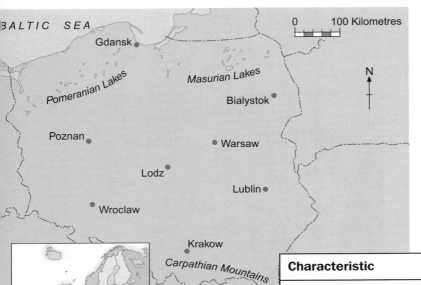

**A** Poland

**B** Warsaw

Poland (map **A**) is the largest of the ten new countries to join the European Union in 2004. Poland is mostly lowland, forming part of the flat area in northern Europe called the North European Plain. To the north lies the Baltic Sea and to the south the Carpathian Mountains.

There are many lakes in Poland, especially in the north east of the country. About 50 per cent of the land area is used to grow crops; the best farmland is in the south west. Forests cover another 30 per cent of the land area. Warsaw is the capital city of Poland (see **B**) and there are several other large cities in the central part of the country.

Table **C** shows how Poland's population and some other characteristics compare with those of the UK (2005).

| Characteristic | Poland | UK |
|---|---|---|
| Total population | 38 620 000 | 60 090 000 |
| Area (km$^2$) | 312 685 | 244 820 |
| Population density (per km$^2$) | 124 | 245 |
| Population who live in urban areas | 63 per cent | 89 per cent |
| Life expectancy<br>Female<br>Male | <br>78 years<br>70 years | <br>80 years<br>75 years |
| Infant mortality rate/1000 births | 9 | 5 |
| Age groups:<br>0–14<br>15–59<br>Over 60 | <br>17 per cent<br>70 per cent<br>13 per cent | <br>8 per cent<br>66 per cent<br>16 per cent |
| Births per thousand people per year | 10 | 11 |
| Deaths per thousand people per year | 10 | 10 |
| Employment:<br>Agriculture<br>Industry<br>Services | <br>27 per cent<br>22 per cent<br>50 per cent | <br>1 per cent<br>25 per cent<br>74 per cent |
| Average annual income per person (US $) | 11 100 | 27 700 |
| People per doctor | 467 | 300 |
| Adult literacy | 99 per cent | 99 per cent |

**C** Characteristics of Poland and the UK

As you can see, Poland has a larger land area than the UK but a smaller population. This means that the population density is much lower than in the UK. In Poland a smaller percentage of people live in towns and cities, too. What differences in the quality of life in the two countries might this lead to? Figure **D** shows some ideas about quality of life.

Access to clean water

Shelter – a home with bathroom, kitchen, heating

Clean safe jobs in industry and services

Good wages

A holiday abroad

Access to TV and computer

Good education and health services

A healthy and varied diet

**D** What do people mean by 'quality of life'?

Life expectancy is only slightly better in the UK, although Poland has far more people per doctor. In Poland the population is younger and has fewer people aged over 60, but the infant mortality rate is higher. More people work in agriculture in Poland, and this may explain the lower average incomes. Will joining the EU change this?

## Activities (S)

1 Study a map of Poland in an atlas.

   a) List the countries that border Poland. Which of these are also members of the EU?

   b) Which sea lies to the north of Poland? Which mountains lie to the south?

2 Look at table **C**.

   a) Give *one* similarity between Poland and the UK.

   b) List *three* differences between Poland and the UK.

   c) Explain why Poland has a lower population density than the UK.

   d) Suggest why the average income of people in Poland is so much lower than that in the UK.

3 a) In small groups, discuss why you think Poland wanted to join the EU. What benefits do you think it will bring? Why might some countries already in the EU be worried about Poland joining the EU? Contribute your ideas to a class discussion.

   b) After the discussion, write a letter to your local MP or newspaper. You can write in support of Poland's membership of the EU or as an EU member worried about the expansion of the EU.

# Who are the Europeans?

**A** An area with low population density

1  Study photograph **A** and draw a sketch of it (see pages 145–155 of *SKILLS in geography* for more help). Label it to show the reasons why it shows a low density of population.

2  Do you think the area in **A** will be in the core or periphery of Europe? Explain the difference between the core and the periphery.

| Country | Birth rate | Death rate | Natural increase |
|---------|-----------|-----------|-----------------|
| France | 12 | 9 | 12 – 9 = 3 |
| UK | 11 | 10 | |
| Germany | 8 | 10 | |
| Ireland | 14 | 8 | |

**B**  Population statistics for some European countries, 2004

3  a) Copy and complete table **B** to show the natural increase in each country.
   b) Which countries have a growing population? Which has a declining population?
   c) Suggest why the population is growing in some countries and declining in others.
   d) Study the following statements. Decide whether each one applies to countries with ageing populations or those with youthful, growing populations. Try to explain each one.
   • We need to make sure we can pay for all of the pensions that are needed.
   • We need to have more schools and nurseries.
   • We will need more migrant workers as the workforce gets smaller.
   • With more children, larger houses will be needed.
   • We need to close children's wards and open more centres to care for the elderly.
   • We should think about raising family allowances so that birth rates go up.

4  **Tops and tails**
   Explain the differences between each of these pairs of words or phrases.
   • *Emigration* and *immigration*
   • *Forced migration* and *voluntary migration*
   • *Population distribution* and *population density*
   • *Refugee* and *economic migrant*
   • *Push factors* and *pull factors*

# >> 3   Europe's weather and climate

**Find the UK on this satellite photograph of Europe. When do you think it might have been taken?**

## *Learning objectives*

What are you going to learn about in this chapter?

> What weather is and how it is measured
> What clouds are and why it rains
> What low and high pressure are
> How and why the weather changes
> How satellite images are used
> The difference between weather and climate
> What the European climates are
> How climate affects our everyday lives

# What is weather?

> Finding out what weather is
> Learning how people measure the weather

Heavy rain clouds

Trees bending show strong winds

People in waterproof clothes suggest rain and damp surroundings

**A** Can we tell what the weather is like by looking?

**B** Weather forecast for the UK, 22 August 2004

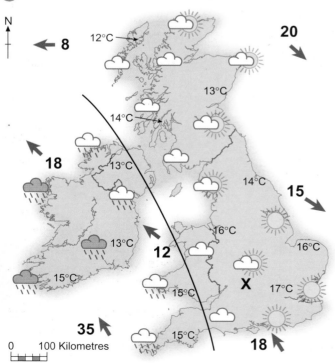

The **weather** is the state of the atmosphere at any moment; it might be wet or dry, snowing or sunny. Everyone is interested in the weather because it affects their everyday lives so much.

## FORECASTING THE WEATHER

You can tell quite a lot about the weather just by looking outside (**A**). You can get more information from a weather forecast, from the radio, TV or in newspapers. Map **B** shows a typical **weather forecast** from a newspaper. Most weather forecasts tell you about the temperature, rainfall, cloud and wind in a place. These are all elements of the weather. **Meteorologists** rely on much more accurate measurements and observations than simply looking outside! This is because they need to prepare a forecast; they have to predict what the weather will be like. This information comes from **weather stations** and instruments carried on planes, ships, weather balloons and satellites. Figure **C** shows some of the instruments used to measure the weather.

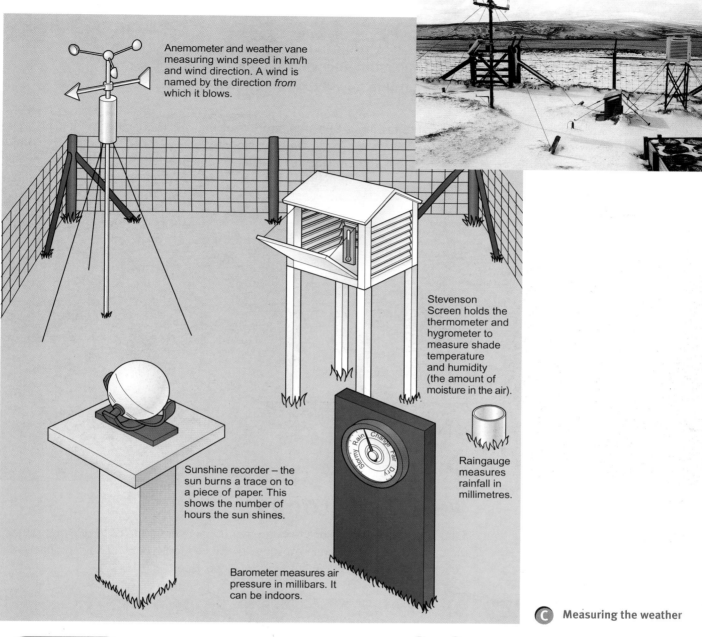

Anemometer and weather vane measuring wind speed in km/h and wind direction. A wind is named by the direction *from* which it blows.

Stevenson Screen holds the thermometer and hygrometer to measure shade temperature and humidity (the amount of moisture in the air).

Raingauge measures rainfall in millimetres.

Sunshine recorder – the sun burns a trace on to a piece of paper. This shows the number of hours the sun shines.

Barometer measures air pressure in millibars. It can be indoors.

 Measuring the weather

## Activities

**1** a) Describe the weather that area X on map **B** is having.

   b) Write a similar weather report for where you are today. You could compare this with the report in your local paper or on the BBC website – use the Hotlinks site (see page 2).

**2** Study map **B**. Make a copy of the weather symbols used on the map and describe what each one means.

**3** Look at **C**. Describe which instruments you would use to measure each of the following:

   a) hours of sunshine

   b) rainfall

   c) temperature.

**4** Write your own definitions for these terms: weather, weather forecast.

### Key words

**Meteorologist** – a person who studies the weather

**Weather** – the state of the atmosphere at any one time: whether it is sunny or raining, cloudy, hot, cold, etc.

**Weather forecast** – a prediction of what the weather will be like

**Weather station** – a place used to record the weather with meteorological instruments

# How and why does the sky change?

## Key words

**Cloud** – millions of tiny water droplets or ice crystals

**Condensation** – when water vapour, a gas, is changed into water as a liquid in water droplets and clouds by cooling

**Convection current** – when warm air rises through the air

**Evaporation** – when water from lakes and seas is changed into water vapour, a gas, by heating

**Front** – the zone where two blocks of air meet

**Precipitation** – all forms of moisture that reach the ground surface, e.g. snow, rain, sleet, dew

**Relief** – the height and shape of the land

**Water cycle** – the movement of water between the air, the oceans and the ground

One minute the sky is blue, the next it is cloudy and eventually it may rain... but why? The answer lies in the **water cycle** – the way water is moved between the ground, the air and the sea creating **clouds** and **precipitation** (**A**).

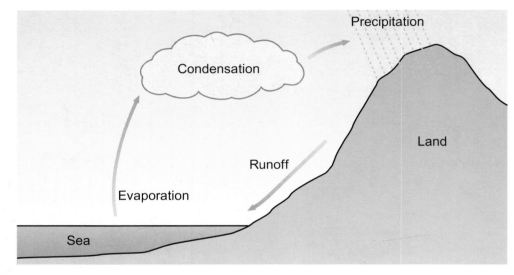

**A** The water cycle

## WHAT ARE CLOUDS?

Clouds are made of millions of tiny water droplets or, in the case of cirrus clouds, ice crystals. The water cycle explains how clouds form, but you have probably noticed that there are different types of cloud (see **B**).

**B** The three cloud types

**Cirrus clouds**   Thin wispy clouds very high in the sky. Temperatures are freezing so the clouds are made of ice crystals. They often mean bad weather is on the way.

**Cumulus clouds**   Fluffy clouds that often rise quite high in the sky. They can bring showers. Some grow into very tall clouds that bring very heavy rain and thunder and lightning.

**Stratus clouds**   Huge blankets of grey cloud often quite low in the sky. They often bring light drizzle.

# WHAT KIND OF RAIN IS IT?

Geographers use the term *precipitation* for all water that reaches the ground surface, such as rainfall, snow, sleet and frost. Rainfall comes from clouds, and clouds form when air carrying water rises. But how does air rise?

When warm air rises, the air is cooled. Cool air cannot hold as much moisture as warm air. So the **water vapour** in the air condenses to form clouds and rainfall. Air can be forced to rise in three ways, so geographers give rain three different names depending on what has caused the air to rise (**C**).

**Key words**

**Water vapour** – water as a gas in the atmosphere
**Wind** – moving air from an area of high pressure to an area of low pressure

## 1 Relief rainfall

**Winds** that blow over the sea pick up moisture. When this moist air reaches high land it can only do one thing: it has to go up. As the air rises it cools and the water vapour it is carrying **condenses** forming clouds and rainfall. The rain is forced to rise because of the **relief** of the land, so this type of rainfall is called *relief rainfall*.

## 2 Convectional rainfall

On very warm days, the sun heats the ground, which heats the air above. The warm air rises as a **convection current**. As the air rises it cools, and the moisture condenses to form clouds and rainfall. Sometimes the convection currents are very strong and they produce very tall clouds and heavy rainfall with thunder and lightning.

## 3 Frontal rainfall

Great blocks of air at different temperatures move around the Earth over sea and land. When warm air and cold air meet, they do not mix. The zone where they meet is called a **front**. At the front the lighter warm air is forced to rise over the colder denser air. The rising air cools and eventually clouds form and rain falls. We call this *frontal rainfall*. The symbols in **D** are used on weather maps to show fronts where the different blocks of air meet.

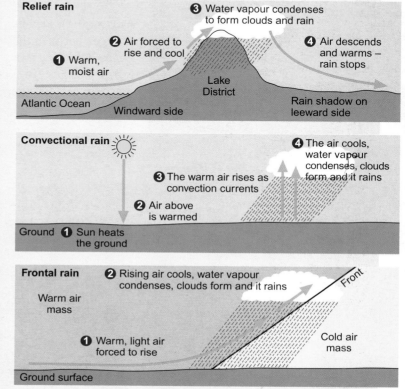

**Relief rain**
❶ Warm, moist air
❷ Air forced to rise and cool
❸ Water vapour condenses to form clouds and rain
❹ Air descends and warms – rain stops
Lake District
Atlantic Ocean
Windward side
Rain shadow on leeward side

**Convectional rain**
❶ Sun heats the ground
❷ Air above is warmed
❸ The warm air rises as convection currents
❹ The air cools, water vapour condenses, clouds form and it rains
Ground

**Frontal rain**
❶ Warm, light air forced to rise
❷ Rising air cools, water vapour condenses, clouds form and it rains
Warm air mass
Cold air mass
Front
Ground surface

**C** The three types of rain

# Activities

(S) (A)

1 Rearrange these sentences so that they are in the correct order to describe what is happening in the water cycle.

A Some of the rain flows into rivers, and some soaks into the land.

B As the air rises, it cools.

C The sun's energy makes water evaporate from the oceans and become water vapour.

D Clouds form and it rains.

E The water vapour in the air condenses.

F The rivers eventually flow back into the oceans.

G The warm air carrying the water vapour rises.

2 In pairs or small groups, produce an illustrated poster to show the life of a water droplet, suitable to give to a pupil in primary school. Think about what words they will understand. How can you make it clear for them?

3 Design *five* questions to test your neighbour on the three different types of rainfall. Take turns to question each other. How did you do?

Warm front
Cold front

**D** Symbols for warm and cold fronts

# Feeling the pressure?

> Understanding air pressure and how it is linked to the weather
> Learning the key facts about anticyclones

The air is pressing down on the Earth's surface, although we cannot feel it. This is **air pressure**. We measure air pressure in **millibars** using a **barometer** (**A**). Pressure is shown on a weather map by **isobars**. An isobar joins together places with the same air pressure, in the same way that a contour line on a map joins together places with the same height.

Air pressure varies from place to place and from time to time. The pressure changes because the temperature of the air changes. Warm air tends to be less dense and rises, giving low pressure. Denser colder air tends to sink and give higher pressure (**B**). Wind is simply air moving from areas of high pressure to areas of low pressure.

 **A** A barometer

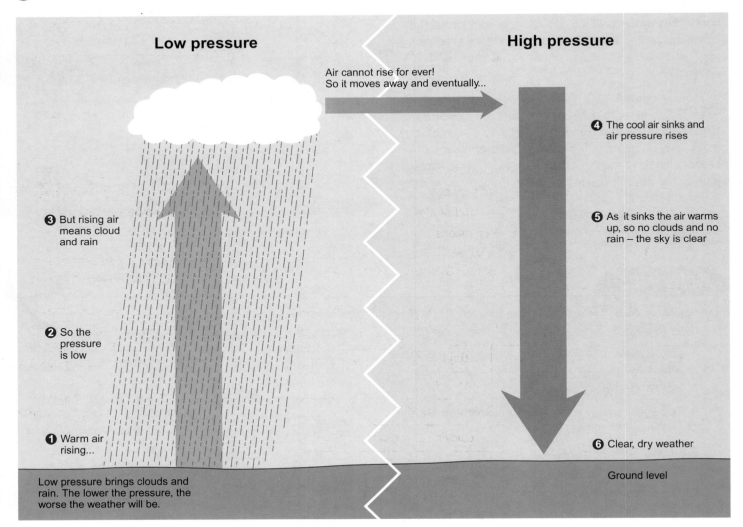

Low pressure

High pressure

Air cannot rise for ever!
So it moves away and eventually...

❹ The cool air sinks and air pressure rises

❸ But rising air means cloud and rain

❺ As it sinks the air warms up, so no clouds and no rain – the sky is clear

❷ So the pressure is low

❶ Warm air rising...

❻ Clear, dry weather

Ground level

Low pressure brings clouds and rain. The lower the pressure, the worse the weather will be.

**B** High and low pressure

## FACT FILE    ANTICYCLONES

Areas of low pressure often bring cloudy and wet weather. An area of low pressure often has a front where air of different temperatures comes together. This is called a **depression**. Areas of high pressure are called **anticyclones**; here the air is sinking and so they bring clear skies and dry weather.

**Key facts: Anticyclones**
- Areas of high pressure
- Air is sinking and warming
- Isobars are far apart so winds are light
- Winds blow clockwise away from the centre
- Skies are usually clear
- Heatwaves in summer
- Cold and frosty in winter, or fog if air is moist

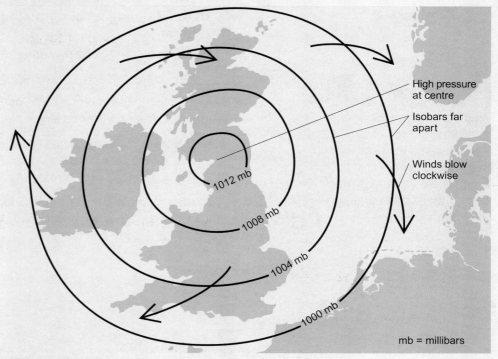

High pressure at centre

Isobars far apart

Winds blow clockwise

1012 mb
1008 mb
1004 mb
1000 mb

mb = millibars

**C** The closer together the isobars are, the stronger the winds

## Activities

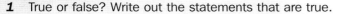

**1** True or false? Write out the statements that are true.

  A Air pressure is measured by a barometer.

  B Contour lines show pressure on a weather map.

  C High-pressure areas are called anticyclones.

  D High-pressure areas have rising air and rainfall.

  E Low-pressure areas are called depressions.

**2** Look at **B**. In groups, describe the weather you get in an area of low pressure and in an area of high pressure. Give some reasons why. Compare notes with the other groups in the class.

**3** Using **C**, complete a table like the one below. Select the correct words so that your table is true for anticyclones.

| Feature | Anticyclones |
|---------|--------------|
| Pressure at the centre | *High or low?* |
| Fronts | *None, 1 or 2?* |
| Wind direction | *Clockwise or anticlockwise?* |
| Wind strength | *Gentle or strong?* |
| Weather in the summer | *Cold and damp or heatwaves?* |
| Weather in the winter | *Cold and frosty or very wet?* |

### Key words

**Air pressure** – the 'weight' of the air pressing down on the Earth's surface

**Anticyclone** – an area of high pressure where winds blow outwards

**Barometer** – instrument used to measure air pressure

**Depression** – a swirling system with low pressure at the centre and fronts

**Isobar** – a line on a weather map that joins together places with the same air pressure

**Millibars** – units used to measure air pressure

# Why does the weather change?

> Understanding what air masses are and how they can be different
> Finding out what happens when a depression passes

## Key words

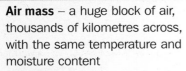

**Air mass** – a huge block of air, thousands of kilometres across, with the same temperature and moisture content

**Atmosphere** – the 'envelope' of air masses that surrounds the Earth

In some parts of Europe, such as the UK, the weather can change quickly. One day it may be bright and sunny and the next cool and wet. This is because the air is constantly moving and is not a single block of air.

The **atmosphere** is made up of huge blocks of air, thousands of kilometres across, called **air masses**. These air masses can be warm or cold, dry or damp depending on where they were formed (**A**).

When different air masses meet they do not mix. The area where the two different air masses meet is called a front (**B**) (see also **D** on page 35). Air rises at a front, causing cloud and rainfall.

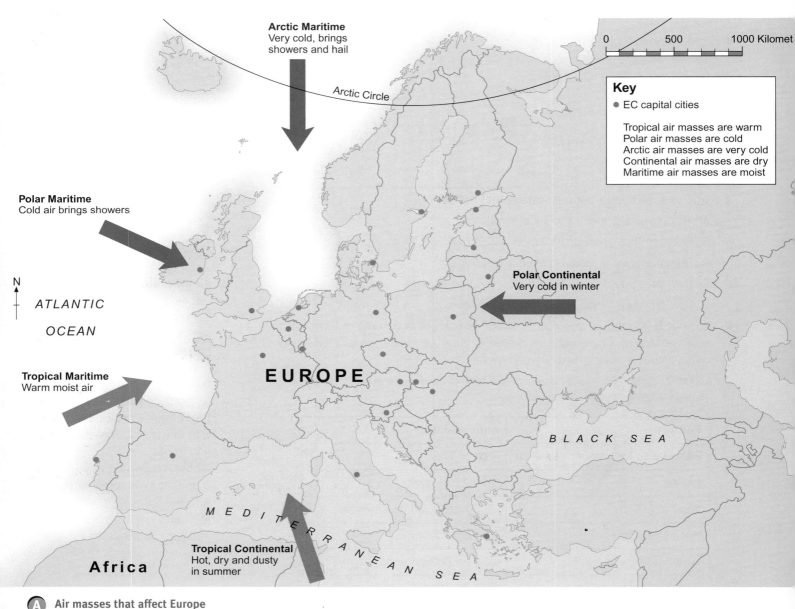

**Arctic Maritime**
Very cold, brings showers and hail

Arctic Circle

0    500    1000 Kilomet

**Key**
● EC capital cities

Tropical air masses are warm
Polar air masses are cold
Arctic air masses are very cold
Continental air masses are dry
Maritime air masses are moist

**Polar Maritime**
Cold air brings showers

**Polar Continental**
Very cold in winter

N

ATLANTIC

OCEAN

**Tropical Maritime**
Warm moist air

EUROPE

BLACK SEA

MEDITERRANEAN SEA

**Tropical Continental**
Hot, dry and dusty in summer

Africa

 **A** Air masses that affect Europe

# THE PASSING OF A DEPRESSION

Depressions are swirling masses of cloud. They have fronts that bring cloud and rainfall. They often bring wet and cloudy weather to the UK and other parts of Europe. At the fronts the warm air rises, causing cloud and rainfall. Figures **C** and **D** show what happens when a depression crosses the UK. You can see that at the warm front there is a long period of quite light rainfall while at the cold front the rainfall is heavier, but lasts for less time.

 **Different types of front**

Where a warmer air mass is behind a colder air mass...

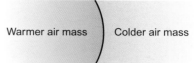

...on a weather map this is shown by a warm front

Where a colder air mass is behind a warmer air mass...

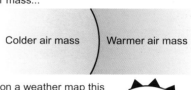

...on a weather map this is shown by a cold front

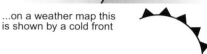

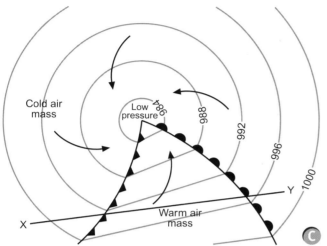

**Fact file: A depression**
- Isobars close together, so strong winds
- Winds blow anticlockwise towards the centre
- Two fronts, a warm and a cold one
- Pressure low at the centre
- Two air masses
- Cloud and rain at the fronts
- Move from west to east across Europe

**C** **Weather map of a depression**

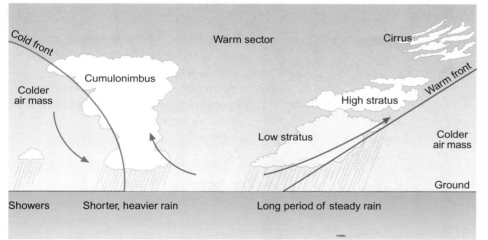

 **Cross-section from X to Y through the depression shown in source C**

## Activities

1 Use map **A** to answer these questions.

a) Which air mass will bring the coldest weather to Europe? Give a reason for your answer.

b) Which air mass will bring the warmest weather to Europe? Why?

c) Which *three* air masses are always damp and likely to bring rain? Give a reason for your answer.

2 Draw and label the symbols for a warm and cold front. Write a sentence below each one to say what weather it brings.

3 Which *three* types of air masses most commonly affect the weather in the UK?

# Satellites help forecast the weather

> Finding out how a satellite works
> Looking at how people use satellite images

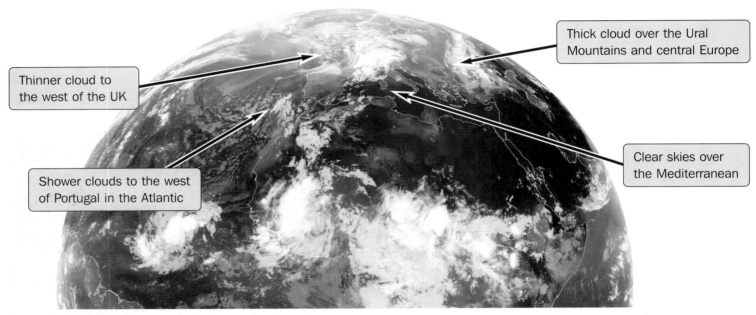

Thinner cloud to the west of the UK

Thick cloud over the Ural Mountains and central Europe

Shower clouds to the west of Portugal in the Atlantic

Clear skies over the Mediterranean

**A** What does an infrared satellite image show?

**B** Infrared satellite image for 6am on 27 October 2000

Out in space there are artificial satellites that take pictures of the Earth several times a day. The pictures are used to help meteorologists prepare weather forecasts (see **A**). Look at these facts about **satellite images**.

- The image is a photograph taken by satellite cameras high above the Earth.
- A camera sends signals to a computer on Earth.
- The computer adds coastlines, lines of longitude and latitude and sometimes colour.
- The image shows the cloud cover at a particular moment.
- On an **infrared** image, areas with no cloud cover appear black, and white areas are dense cloud.
- Infrared images can be taken at any time of day or night because they use heat, not light.
- Visible images can only be taken during daylight hours.

# THE STORMS OF OCTOBER 2000

Meteorologists were able to forecast the severe weather that was to hit Britain, but that didn't seem to stop the chaos that followed (see **B** and **C**)!

Image **B** shows a very deep depression in the north-west Atlantic. The depression was moving westwards, and over the next few days three smaller 'daughter' depressions swept over the UK. They brought heavy rain, strong winds and **tornadoes**. Areas were flooded, buildings damaged and trees brought down which blocked roads and railways. The article in **C** tells some of the story.

## STORMS LASH BRITAIN

The worst storms in a decade have battered southern Britain, killing three people and flooding roads and towns

Winds reaching almost 100mph brought travel chaos, prompting Railtrack to close stations across the region and bringing a warning to motorists to stay at home.

Hundreds of houses have been evacuated and fallen trees have caused damage to power lines.

The port of Dover was closed for several hours, but most services had resumed by Monday afternoon. Thousands of passengers had been stranded mid-Channel waiting for the winds to die down.

Huge waves burst over the promenade at Dover

**C** Newspaper report, 30 October 2000. Reproduced from BBC News at bbcnews.co.uk

## Activities

1   Look at satellite image **A**. Discuss the image as a class. Which parts will the satellite camera have taken and which have been added? What do the black areas represent? Can different types of cloud be seen? Where might it be raining?

2   Use the Hotlinks site to visit the Meteosat website of The Meteorological Office. Study the satellite image for the UK today. What does it show? Compare the image with the sky outside your classroom and a newspaper report of the weather for the day. Are there any similarities and differences? Try to explain why they might be different.

3   **The storms of October 2000**

   a) Using satellite image **B**, draw a sketch to show the main areas of cloud cover shown. Add the following labels in the correct places on your map:

   thick cloud    thin cloud    clear skies    likely to be raining
   rain showers    edge of the photograph from the satellite
   warm front    cold front

   b) How was your region affected by the storms of October 2000? Access the BBC News website for 31 October 2000 via Hotlinks to find out. Draw a sketch map of your local region and add labels to show the damage caused by the storm.

4   Imagine you were caught up in the storms of 2000. Write a diary entry for October 2000 describing what happened and how you felt. Perhaps you have a true story of your own to tell.

## Key words

**Infrared** – radiation that is similar to light but invisible to humans; it can be used in photography
**Satellite image** – a photograph taken by a satellite camera high above the Earth's surface
**Tornado** – a rapidly moving and vicious spiral of air that is smaller than a hurricane

# Europe's climates

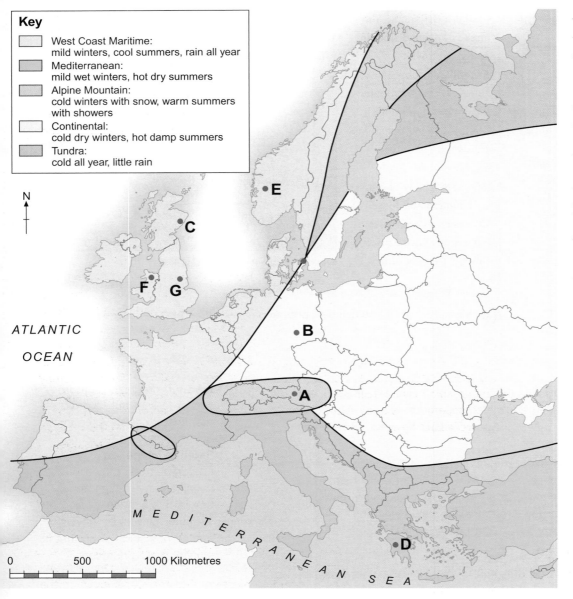

**Key**

- West Coast Maritime: mild winters, cool summers, rain all year
- Mediterranean: mild wet winters, hot dry summers
- Alpine Mountain: cold winters with snow, warm summers with showers
- Continental: cold dry winters, hot damp summers
- Tundra: cold all year, little rain

N

ATLANTIC OCEAN

MEDITERRANEAN SEA

0    500    1000 Kilometres

 Europe's climate zones

The weather is the state of the atmosphere at any one time, and as you have learned, it can change from hour to hour. The **climate**, on the other hand, is the average weather of a place. It is worked out by taking the average of weather measurements over a long time, often more than 30 years. Places with similar climates are grouped together to produce climate zones. Map **A** shows these climatic zones in Europe. A general pattern can be noticed:

- it is colder in the north than in the south
- it is wetter in the west than in the east
- upland areas, e.g. the Alps, are colder than lowland areas
- the Mediterranean region has the hottest and driest weather in Europe.

## WHY DO DIFFERENT CLIMATES EXIST?

### The effect of latitude

The further north you travel in Europe, the further from the Equator and the heating effect of the sun you go. So countries further north are cooler than those further south because they receive less energy from the sun. The sun's rays have to travel further through the atmosphere and heat a larger land area.

**The effect of latitude**

Edge of atmosphere

Longer distance through atmosphere

Larger surface to heat

EARTH

SUN

0°

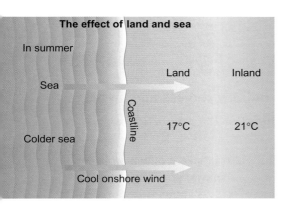

The effect of land and sea

In summer

Sea

Land | Inland

Colder sea

Coastline

17°C | 21°C

Cool onshore wind

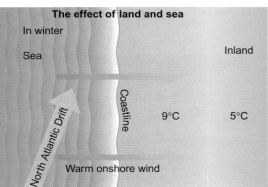

The effect of land and sea

In winter

Sea

Inland

Coastline

9°C | 5°C

North Atlantic Drift

Warm onshore wind

## The effect of land and sea

In summer, coastal areas are cooler than those inland. This is because the sea is cooler than the land in summer and **onshore winds** cool the land down. The reverse happens in the winter because the sea is warmer than the land so coastal areas are often warmer. In western Europe this is helped by the warm ocean current – the **North Atlantic Drift**.

The effect of altitude

0°C — 1600 m

1200 m

800 m

400 m

0

10°C

## The effect of altitude (height above sea level)

As you climb up a mountain it often feels colder. This is because temperature falls as altitude increases. The temperature falls by about 1.6°C for every 100 metres.

## The effect of winds

Winds that have blown over land are dry and bring dry weather to the area they blow over. Winds that have blown over the sea have picked up water and are moist. They often bring rain to areas they blow over. In Europe some countries are affected by the westerly winds. These have blown over the Atlantic Ocean and are moist. This explains why countries in the west of Europe are often wetter than those in the east.

## Activities

1   What is the difference between weather and climate?

2   Decide whether each of the following statements describes the climate or the weather of an area.

   A  The match was cancelled because of heavy rain on Saturday.

   B  It is usually very hot and dry in Greece in the summer.

   C  We always ski in Switzerland in the winter when it is cold enough for snow.

   D  In August 2004 Boscastle was badly flooded by a terrible rainstorm.

   E  We walked along the beach at Scarborough on Wednesday because it was fine.

   F  We avoid going to Scotland in August because it usually rains a lot.

3   Look at places A–G on map **A**. In small groups, select *one* of the statements below and produce an overhead transparency to explain the statement – your answer should include a diagram. Present your findings to the class using the overhead projector.

   • A is cooler than B although it is further south.

   • E is the coldest of all the places shown.

   • F receives high rainfall, higher than G.

   • F is warmer than G in winter but colder than G in summer.

   • D is very hot and dry in summer.

   • C is cooler than G at all times of the year.

# How does the climate affect us?

> Exploring how climate affects holiday choices and farming
> Learning to draw climate graphs

The climate affects the lives of every one of us. For example, it affects what we wear, what we eat, the sorts of houses we live in, where we go on holiday (see **A** and **B**) and what we do in our free time. It also affects us in other ways – when we put on the central heating and when we put an extra duvet on the bed. Look at the annual rainfall and temperatures for London and Bergen in northern Europe (**C**).

**A** Where in Europe would you expect to find this scene?

**B** What kind of holiday would you expect here?

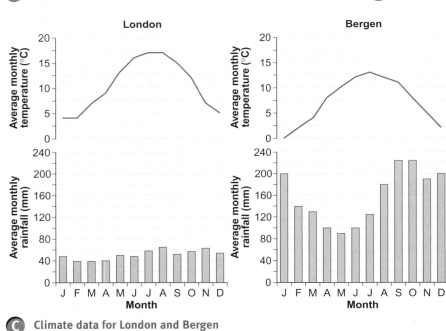

**C** Climate data for London and Bergen

**D** A crop of oranges, ready for picking

All kinds of activities are influenced by climate. Farmers have to think about what grows best in their local climate as well.

- Orange trees grow best where there are hot, dry summers and mild, wet winters (see **D**). Spring frosts can ruin the blossom.

- Hay can grow in a wide variety of climates, including quite cold and wet climates.
- Wheat can survive in a variety of climates but grows best where summers are hot to ripen the grain and there are showers of rain.

However, there can still be disasters. In some years late frosts can ruin the blossom on fruit trees. In 2004, the grain harvests of many UK farmers were destroyed by long periods of cool and wet weather.

## Activities

**1** a) Look at photos **A** and **B**. Match each house to one of the numbered locations marked on map **A** on page 42. Draw a sketch of the house and label the features to show how it suits the climate.

   b) *Either* draw a sketch of the building you live in *or* use a photograph of a house that would be found in the UK. Show how it is adapted to suit the climate in the UK.

**2** Look at photo **D** and map **A** (page 42). Where in Europe would you expect oranges to be grown? Give reasons for your choices.

**3** a) Look at the *SKILLS* box and draw a climate graph for Athens using the table below.

| Athens | J | F | M | A | M | J | J | A | S | O | N | D |
|---|---|---|---|---|---|---|---|---|---|---|---|---|
| **Temperature (°C)** | 8 | 11 | 16 | 23 | 27 | 31 | 30 | 24 | 17 | 11 | 9 | 7 |
| **Rainfall (mm)** | 48 | 39 | 30 | 25 | 25 | 15 | 10 | 12 | 13 | 43 | 70 | 70 |

   b) Read Alexis's story below. Now make your graph into a living graph for Alexis by adding labels for each activity at the correct time of the year (see pages 145–155 of *SKILLS in geography*).

I live in Athens – the climate certainly affects what I do at different times of the year.

A Temperature has fallen below 10°C. Time to get out my long trousers and sweatshirts.

B A really hot weekend – time to go to the beach for a swim.

C Temperatures are getting high – over 20°C – need to stock up on anti-mosquito cream and suntan lotion.

D Temperatures are below 10°C – time to holiday somewhere hot, perhaps Malaysia or South Africa this year.

E Summer is here – great! I can wear shorts for school. Home-grown melons and peaches are in the shops.

F It's really cool this week – we've had the heating on.

**4** Complete a calendar of your activities during the year to show how climate affects your life. Draw a climate graph for where you live and create your own living graph. Try to include the foods you eat, your activities, the clothes you wear and holidays you might go on at different times of the year.

### SKILLS

**How to draw a climate graph**

1 Draw graph axes like those in **C**.
2 Allow 12 cm on the horizontal axis for twelve months. Label these J, F, M, etc.
3 Put a scale for rainfall on the lower part of the vertical axis.
4 Above this put a scale for temperature.
5 Plot the monthly rainfall figures as a bar graph.
6 Plot the monthly temperature figures as a line graph. Place each cross or dot in the middle of the column because it is the average temperature for the month.
7 Add a title and label the axes.

*For more help* see page 148 of *SKILLS in geography*

# Choosing where to go on holiday

| Capital city | July | | November | |
|---|---|---|---|---|
| | Temp. (°C) | Weather | Temp. (°C) | Weather |
| London | 14 | Thunderstorms | 7 | Cloudy |
| Dublin | 12 | Rain | 8 | Rain |
| Paris | 15 | Cloudy | 4 | Rain |
| Amsterdam | 15 | Thunderstorms | 6 | Cloudy |
| Brussels | 15 | Cloudy | 6 | Cloudy |
| Luxembourg City | 13 | Fair | 5 | Cloudy |
| Madrid | 23 | Sunny | 8 | Cloudy |
| Lisbon | 25 | Sunny | 14 | Sunny |
| Rome | 25 | Fair | 13 | Fair |
| Athens | 30 | Sunny | 18 | Fair |
| Berlin | 15 | Sunny | 2 | Sleet |
| Copenhagen | 13 | Showers | −1 | Snow |

 **A**  What's the weather like in Europe?

It's January, and the Carter family are deciding what to do about their family holiday this year.

**Mr Carter**
I don't like it too hot, I come out in a rash. I would like to do some walking in nice scenery and play golf. I like to go somewhere where there are places of interest to visit. I like Italian food.

**Mrs Carter**
I want to relax in some sunshine. I don't mind the odd day trip to see the sights and do some shopping. The shorter the flight is, the better. I enjoy good food and wine.

**Michael Carter (14 years)**
We'll have to go in the school holidays, anyway it's hotter then. I would like to go where there is a beach and lots of water sports – I'd like to learn to scuba dive and I like theme parks. I don't like foreign food and I hate sightseeing and shopping.

**Helen Carter (17 years)**
I am doing Art A level and I'd like to visit one of Europe's big art galleries. I also want to have a good time – somewhere with a nice beach would be good.

**B**  The Carter family

1   Make a key for the different weather symbols needed to show the weather in table **A**.

2   Look at **B** and the map that your teacher will give you showing the capital cities of Europe. Where should the Carter family go on holiday?

Work in a group of four. Each person takes the part of one of the Carter family. In role, discuss where is best for your holiday and come to a decision in your group about where and when to go. Present your decision to the rest of the class. Where should the family go, when and why? Did the climate for your choice influence your decision?

• Who will be happy with your choice of the holiday, and why?

• Who will be least happy about the holiday choice, and why?

# >> 4 Tourism – good or bad?

**Why do people like visiting places like this?**

**How do the people who live here feel about tourism?**

## *Learning objectives*

What are you going to learn about in this chapter?

> What tourism is
> How and why tourism is important
> What changes are taking place in the tourist industry
> Different types of holidays
> Whether tourism is good or bad
> How tourism can be managed

 **Costa Blanca, Spain**

# What is tourism?

> Finding out what tourists and tourism are
> Understanding the growth of tourism

Most people think of summer holidaymakers when they hear the word, but almost anyone who travels anywhere at any time may be a **tourist**. People who stay away from home for a short time for business, to visit relatives or for other purposes are all tourists. Tourists may stay within their own country (**domestic tourism**) or they may travel abroad (**international tourism**). Tourists, hotels, airports, coach drivers and souvenir sellers are all part of the tourism industry.

Fieldwork abroad – brilliant! I hope the assignment goes well.

The shopping is supposed to be fantastic!

I am so looking forward to meeting my grandson for the first time.

I've an important business meeting tomorrow.

Looking forward to visiting all of those historic sites!

Can't wait to be on that beach!

I hope my presentation goes down well at the conference.

 **A** What is a tourist?

Tourism is the fastest growing industry in the world (**B**). Tourism has grown so much because:

- people have more days of paid holiday
- people take more holidays during the year
- transport has improved, e.g. long-distance flights, cheap airlines
- large multinational companies require more national and international business travel
- there is more information about different countries and cultures on TV and the Internet
- people are wealthier and can afford to travel
- pensioners are younger and better off
- **package holidays** have made travelling abroad easier.

But not all parts of the world benefit equally. Table **C** shows the top ten destinations for tourists.

## Key words

**Package holiday** – an all-inclusive deal from a travel agent; the package usually includes travel, accommodation, food and some entertainment

**Tourism** – the industry that caters for visitors

**Tourist** – a person who travels away from home for a short time and intends to return home afterwards

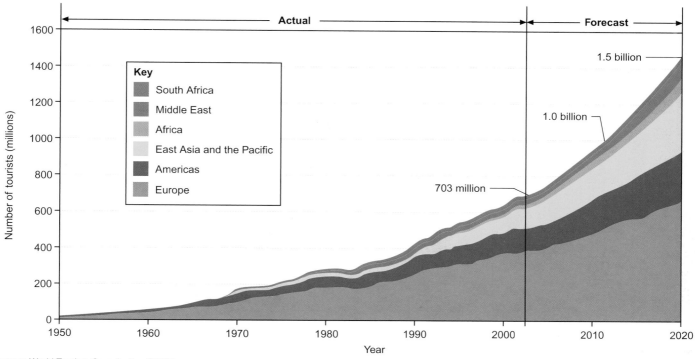

Source: World Tourism Organization (WTO)

**B** How has global tourism changed?

## Activities

**1** a) In pairs, list all the types of holiday you can think of. Think of the holidays and trips that you, your families and friends have been on. These definitions of holidays may help you:

package    independent    sports
short break    activity

   b) As a class, put your lists together. How many different kinds of holidays did you think of? What makes each of these trips seem like a holiday?

**2** Study **B**.

   a) How many tourists are predicted for 2020?

   b) Describe what has happened to the numbers of tourists over time.

   c) Rank the regions according to the numbers of tourists in 2004.

   d) In pairs, discuss why you think some regions get more tourists than others. Complete two lists with the following titles:

   • Why some places have many tourists

   • Why some places don't have many tourists

| Rank | Country | Millions of tourists |
|------|---------|----------------------|
| 1 | France | 75.0 |
| 2 | Spain | 52.5 |
| 3 | United States | 40.4 |
| 4 | Italy | 39.6 |
| 5 | China | 33.0 |
| 6 | United Kingdom | 24.8 |
| 7 | Austria | 19.1 |
| 8 | Mexico | 18.7 |
| 9 | Germany | 18.4 |
| 10 | Canada | 17.5 |

**C** The top ten destinations for tourists (2003)

**3** Study **C**.

   a) Draw a bar graph to show the figures in **C** (see pages 145–155 of *SKILLS in geography*). Group the countries by colour and continent. For example, all countries in North America could be orange.

   b) Describe the pattern of the top ten countries. Is it what you would expect? Are there any surprises?

# Tourism – just how important is it?

> Understanding how and why tourism is important
> Patterns of boom and bust in the tourist industry

## FACT FILE  THE WORLD TOURISM INDUSTRY

In 2002, countries worldwide earned over US $500 billion from tourism and over 200 million people worked in the tourism industry. About 700 million tourists were moved around the world. Tourism is one of the largest industries in the world.

In some countries tourism is the largest industry and employer (see **A**). Tourism is one of the top five money-earners in over 80 per cent of countries, so it is very important to keep the tourists coming. You can see how countries earn money from tourism in **B**.

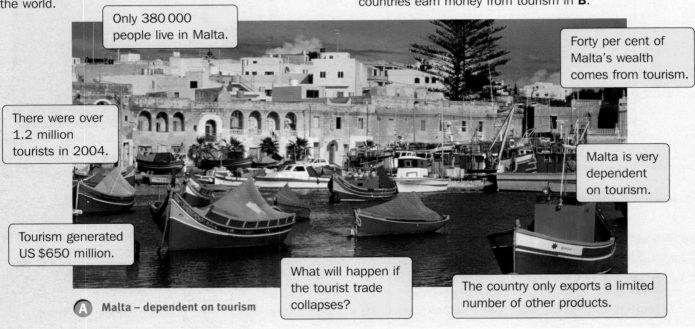

Only 380 000 people live in Malta.

Forty per cent of Malta's wealth comes from tourism.

There were over 1.2 million tourists in 2004.

Malta is very dependent on tourism.

Tourism generated US $650 million.

What will happen if the tourist trade collapses?

The country only exports a limited number of other products.

**A** Malta – dependent on tourism

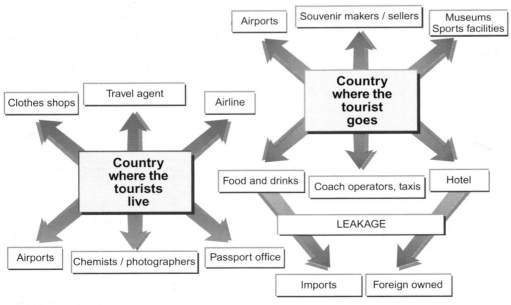

**B** Who benefits from tourism?

## WHO BENEFITS FROM TOURISM?

Tourism is a **service industry** and employs many people in transport, hotels, catering and recreation. Many of these jobs only last for the tourist season and people are unemployed at other times of the year. This is called **seasonal unemployment**. People have little job security and may not get the same job next year. They often have no pension and no training. Seasonal unemployment is a real problem in countries or resorts that have many tourists. So, looking at **B**, who benefits from tourism?

Tourism is especially important in the poorer countries of the world (see table **C**). But not all these countries have a large and successful tourist industry, while others may see a sudden fall in the numbers of tourists to their country.

## WHAT ATTRACTS TOURISTS?

Countries with a successful tourist industry usually offer natural **physical attractions** for visitors, such as the climate, beaches, rainforests and mountains. They may also offer **human attractions** such as historic buildings, theme parks, sporting facilities and cultural events (**D**). Countries with few natural and human attractions benefit little from the tourist industry.

## WHAT ARE THE PROBLEMS?

Even successful tourist industries suddenly see visitor numbers drop. Reasons may include:

- Political, e.g. bombing in Israel and the 9/11 disaster in New York
- Natural, e.g. hurricanes in the Caribbean
- Medical, e.g. the SARS outbreak in Nepal
- Fashion: other countries become more fashionable
- Facilities, e.g. in Benidorm facilities and hotels did not keep pace with modern demands.

Changes like these can be disastrous, especially for poor countries that rely so much on the tourist industry.

| Country | % population living on below US $1 a day | % of country's income (GDP) coming from tourism |
|---|---|---|
| Nigeria | 70 | 2 |
| The Gambia | 54 | 11 |
| Honduras | 41 | 10.6 |
| Ghana | 39 | 8.4 |
| Nepal | 38 | 7.7 |

 **Tourism earns money in poorer countries**

 **A booming tourist industry**

## Activities

1 Investigate your local area. What are the physical and human attractions for tourists where you live? Produce a short ICT presentation to show the attractions a family might enjoy on a visit to your home area.

2 The SARS virus affected Nepal's tourist industry in 2003. What else has damaged Nepal's tourist industry in recent years?

3 Read the statements below. Which ones would cause a rise in the UK tourist industry and which would cause a decline? In each case explain your answer.
   A London winning the bid for the 2012 Olympic Games
   B A terrorist attack in London
   C The collapse of British Airways
   D The opening of Legoland
   E Climate change – the UK becomes warmer and sunnier.

### Key words

**Human attractions** – facilities for tourists built by people
**Physical attractions** – natural features that attract tourists, e.g. climate, rivers, mountains
**Seasonal unemployment** – when jobs are only available for part of the year, leaving people without work at other times
**Service industry** – industry where people provide a service instead of making a product

# Europe's tourist attractions

> ## Looking at different types of holidays in Europe
> ## Learning how to draw compound bars

**Sun, sand and sea**

The largest group of tourists are people on holiday. Have you ever been abroad for your holiday? Fifty years ago the answer from most people would have been no! Today more and more people are going abroad. From the UK many people travel to other countries in the European Union. Over 40 per cent of tourists from all over the world visit countries in the European Union, including the UK. The photographs in **A** show some of Europe's most popular tourist destinations. They show the four main types of holiday destinations:

- sun, sand and sea
- winter sports
- scenic – mountains and lakes
- cultural and historic.

**Winter sports**

**Scenic**

**Cultural and historic**

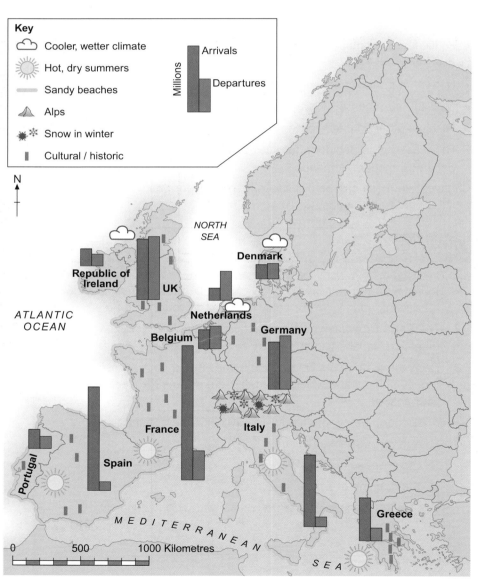

**Key**

- Cooler, wetter climate
- Hot, dry summers
- Sandy beaches
- Alps
- Snow in winter
- Cultural / historic

Millions — Arrivals / Departures

N

NORTH SEA

Denmark

Republic of Ireland

UK

ATLANTIC OCEAN

Netherlands

Belgium

Germany

France

Italy

Portugal

Spain

Greece

MEDITERRANEAN SEA

0    500    1000 Kilometres

Ⓐ **Types of holiday destinations in Europe**

Ⓑ **Arrivals and departures of tourists in some EU countries**

The map in **B** shows the climates and locations for different types of holidays in the European Union. Notice how the climate is colder and wetter further north – snow is highly likely in the winter, especially on higher ground. Further south the climate becomes warmer and drier, especially in summer. Around the Mediterranean Sea summers are particularly hot and dry and there are many beaches. The Alps and Pyrenees are popular for winter sports and also as scenic summer holiday destinations. Most European countries offer some cultural and historic attractions, many located within the large cities, like the Tower of London. The map also shows the relative number of arrivals and departures from countries within the EU. Notice how some countries have more departures than arrivals, such as France, while others have many more arrivals than departures, such as Spain and Greece.

## SKILLS

### How to draw a block bar graph

1 Draw vertical and horizontal axes.
2 Draw bars for one set of values.
3 Above them draw bars for the second set of values, and so on.
4 Colour in each of the divisions and add a key.
5 Label the axes and add a title.

*For more help* see page 150 of *SKILLS in geography*

## Activities

**1** Conduct a survey to find out your class's main holiday destinations last year. Into which categories of holiday do they fit?

   a) Complete a table like the one below to show the results. You can add other countries to the lists.

| Country | Holiday type | | | |
|---|---|---|---|---|
| | Sea and sand | Cultural | Winter sports | Scenic |
| UK | | | | |
| Other EU countries: | | | | |
| France | | | | |
| | | | | |
| | | | | |
| Non-EU countries: | | | | |
| USA | | | | |
| | | | | |
| | | | | |

   b) On an outline map of the world, plot block bar graphs (see the *SKILLS* box) to show the number of people who visited each country and the type of holiday. Add a key for the colours used.

   c) Which were the least and the most popular destinations? Try to explain why.

   d) Which were the least and most popular types of holidays? Explain why.

**2** Study the photographs in **A**. In small groups, choose *one* of the photographs and describe what it shows and what activities tourists could do in the area. Suggest what type of holiday is being shown and a possible location for the photograph in the European Union.

**3** a) Using map **B**, produce *two* lists: those countries that receive more tourist arrivals than departures and those that have fewer arrivals than departures.

   b) In small groups, discuss why some countries have more arrivals than departures while others have more departures than arrivals. Contribute your ideas to a class discussion. Write up your findings in a few paragraphs.

# UK tourism

> **Finding out how tourism has changed in the UK**

> **Understanding why patterns of tourism change in the UK**

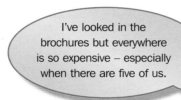

*Source: United Kingdom Tourism Survey 2003*

 **Holidays taken by UK residents**

More and more people in the UK go on holiday every year, and where they are going is changing too (see **A**). Fewer people take holidays in the UK and more are choosing to travel abroad. Notice how the lines on the graph go up and down. Some years the numbers of holidays go down. Look at **B** – this shows there are lots of different reasons.

> I've looked in the brochures but everywhere is so expensive – especially when there are five of us.

> You won't get me on a plane, not with all those terrorists about.

> I lost my job and can't afford a holiday.

> Interest rates have gone up, so the mortgage costs more. It will take me longer to save up for a holiday.

> Last year the summer was really hot – I'll try staying at home this year.

**B** **Going abroad? Not this year...**

Although holidays are on the increase there are still a large percentage of people who have no holiday (34 per cent in 2003). The increase seems to come from people who are taking more than one holiday abroad each year.

Europe is still a very popular destination for UK holidaymakers, but people are also beginning to travel further and to more exotic locations (see **C**). Modern aircraft can travel long distances and competition has made air fares cheaper, so long-haul travel is more attractive now.

However, UK holidays are still popular. Look at the data for 2003 in **D–F**. This shows some of the characteristics of UK tourism.

| Country | People who stayed four nights or more (%) |
|---|---|
| Spain | 27.5 |
| France | 20.2 |
| USA | 7.0 |
| Greece | 5.3 |
| Italy | 4.0 |
| Portugal | 3.6 |
| Irish Republic | 3.5 |
| Turkey | 3.0 |
| Netherlands | 2.7 |
| Cyprus | 2.6 |
| Belgium | 2.3 |
| Germany | 1.8 |
| Malta | 1.3 |
| Austria | 1.3 |
| Other countries | 13.9 |

*Source: United Kingdom Tourism Survey 2003*

 **Where UK residents took their foreign holidays**

| Purpose of trip | Millions of trips |
|---|---|
| Holiday, pleasure/leisure | 70.5 |
| Visiting friends and relatives, mainly as a holiday | 20.5 |
| Business | 22.3 |
| Visiting friends and relatives | 34.3 |
| Other | 3.4 |
| All purposes | 151.0 |

Source: United Kingdom Tourism Survey 2003

**D** **Purpose of tourism in the UK in 2003 for UK residents**

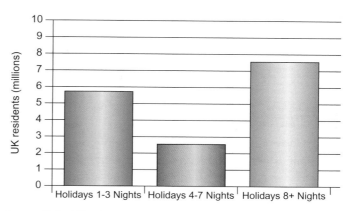

Source: United Kingdom Tourism Survey 2003

**E** **How long UK residents stay**

# Activities

(S) 📄

**1** Look at **A**.

a) Describe the overall trends for:

- the total number of holidays taken
- holidays in Britain
- holidays abroad.

b) In pairs or small groups try to think of reasons why:

- the total number of holidays has increased
- the number of holidays abroad has increased
- why the lines are not straight but go up and down.

**2** Look at **C**.

a) Suggest some countries that may be part of the 'other countries' category.

b) Suggest why Spain and France are very popular with UK tourists. Why are they more popular than Greece or Belgium?

**3** Look at **D–F**.

a) What is the most important purpose of tourism in the UK?

b) Visiting friends and relatives comes a close second. What advantages does this have for people wanting a break?

c) What are the most popular length of stay and the most popular mode of travel? Suggest reasons.

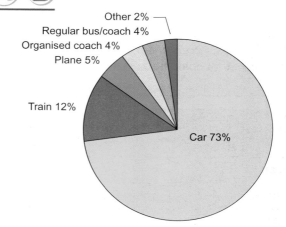

Source: United Kingdom Tourism Survey 2003

 **How UK tourists travelled**

**4** Create the profile of a typical British tourist by completing the table below. Then think about the sort of holiday they would go on. Imagine this tourist lives in your local area and suggest some trips the tourist would make that fit this profile. Explain why the trips would be ideal for your typical tourist.

| | |
|---|---|
| Most important purpose of tourism | |
| Most frequent length of stay | |
| The type of transport most tourists use | |

# Visiting an island in Europe: Menorca

> Finding out about Menorca's attractions for the tourist
> Looking at the problems and future of Menorca's tourist industry

## FACT FILE    MENORCA

Menorca is the second largest island (after Majorca) in the Spanish Balearic Islands. It offers a variety of attractions for the tourist (map **A**). There are numerous coves and bays with sandy beaches (**B**). Sixty per cent of Menorca's population live in the two main towns: Ciutadella, the island's old capital, and Mahon, the new capital where the airport is located. The island is famous for its cheese, wine and leather goods. Sites of historic interest are dotted around the island. Inland the landscape is quite hilly, with farmland, pine forests and small market towns. The island also has its share of human attractions such as fiestas (**C**), golf courses, a water park, equestrian centres and of course shops, hotels and restaurants. You can find out more about Menorca by using Hotlinks (see page 2).

**B** A cove in Menorca

**C** Fiesta horses in Alayor

Menorca is relatively unspoiled. The local authorities have tried hard to resist the development of mass tourism, with its high-rise hotels and concrete jungles. But tourism is going through a difficult time. The number of tourists visiting the island is falling because of:

- International terrorism
- Economic problems in Germany and Italy
- Cheap flights making short-stay holidays attractive
- Improving weather in other parts of Europe – people stay at home
- Low prices in other countries, especially poorer ones, make them cheaper to visit.

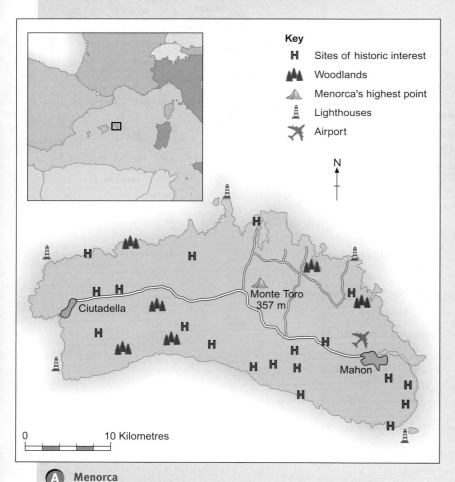

**Key**

| H | Sites of historic interest |
|---|---|
| 🌲🌲 | Woodlands |
| 🔺 | Menorca's highest point |
| 🗼 | Lighthouses |
| ✈ | Airport |

N

Ciutadella

Monte Toro
357 m

Mahon

0        10 Kilometres

**A** Menorca

There are plans in Menorca to:

- enlarge the airport at a cost of 66 million Euros
- make the one main road across the island into a dual carriageway at a cost of 234 million Euros
- build more golf courses.

But these changes are not welcomed by everyone. Look at the comments in **D**.

A bigger airport will mean more planes, more people and more traffic – disturbing the peace and causing more pollution.

Golf courses won't attract that many more tourists, and they eat up huge areas of land. They also need huge amounts of water – one thing Menorca has not got.

The larger road will be ugly – there are already three accidents a day on it.

**D** Views on development in Menorca

Menorca has no energy resources of its own, although a few wind turbines have been built. Tourism puts pressure on the water and energy resources of the island. In recent years visitors have demanded air-conditioning – another drain on electricity supplies. Water supplies are restricted and everyone is asked to conserve supplies in the summer. In Menorca the season is also very short and many locals suffer seasonal unemployment (see **E**).

Until this year I worked in the airport, driving the tourist buses from the aircraft to the terminal building. I hated it – it was so hot and monotonous and the shifts were tiring. The really hard thing was that the tourists only come from April to October; after that there was no job. In the winter I had no money. I tried to get a job as a postman and also thought about training to be a driving instructor. But this year I have a new job. I am still driving, but at one of the holiday complexes. I drive the free bus around the complex and to the beach and the shops. It is much better. You can speak to people and get to know them while they are visiting. I have had some nice tips. I am also hoping that they will keep me on in the winter to help with maintenance jobs, painting the chalets and so on.

**E** Santiago was born and lives in Menorca – he tells you about his work

## Activities

**1** Should Menorca try to increase its tourist numbers? Work in pairs or small groups. Imagine you are in charge of tourism in Menorca. You have been asked to produce a report on the future. Write about:
- whether tourism should grow, stay the same or decrease on Menorca
- the advantages and disadvantages of your plans.

Produce your report using ICT and include maps and diagrams.

**2** Use Hotlinks (see page 2) to find out where Menorca's water supplies come from. Why would building more golf courses increase the consumption of water in Menorca? Try to think of other reasons why residents in Menorca might not want more golf courses.

**3** a) Look at **E**. What are the disadvantages of the jobs Santiago has had?

b) Why would being a postman or driving instructor be better?

c) Many young people leave islands like Menorca because they cannot find a permanent job. What are the disadvantages of this for an island like Menorca?

# Visiting a poorer country: Jamaica

> Finding out why tourism is so important to Jamaica
> Learning about eco-tourism in Jamaica

## FACT FILE    JAMAICA

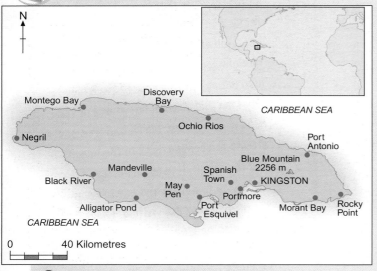

**A** Jamaica – a tropical paradise

Jamaica (map **A**) is an island in the Caribbean Sea, south of Cuba. The island is mountainous in the interior – the highest point is the Blue Mountain peak at 2256 metres above sea level. The narrow coastal plain has many sandy beaches. The climate is tropical – hot all year round but also humid (**B**). There is the threat of hurricanes, especially from July to November, although very few hit.

The island is popular for its beaches and water sports, but also attracts bird-watchers. Jamaica is home to 2.7 million people – 20 per cent live below the poverty line. About one-third of Jamaica's population live in Kingston, the capital.

The island earns most of its money from tourism and the export of **bauxite**. Tourism employs over 75 000 Jamaicans directly and 225 000 indirectly. Over 1 million tourists visit Jamaica every year. In 2000, the best year on record, 1.8 million visitors came, mostly from North America and Europe.

|  | J | F | M | A | M | J | J | A | S | O | N | D |
|---|---|---|---|---|---|---|---|---|---|---|---|---|
| **Rainfall (mm)** | 29 | 24 | 23 | 39 | 104 | 96 | 46 | 107 | 126 | 181 | 95 | 40 |
| **Temp (°C)** | 30 | 30 | 31 | 31 | 32 | 32 | 33 | 32 | 32 | 32 | 31 | 31 |

**B** Jamaica's climate

*Source: www.wordtravels.com*

However, the industry is not stable and the tourist trade plummeted after 9/11. The island also has some problems for tourists: crime and drugs in some areas, harassment by food and souvenir sellers on the beaches, and the upsetting sight of **shanty towns** in Kingston.

## FACT FILE    HOW HAVE JAMAICANS DEVELOPED THEIR TOURISM?

Since 1999 a new master plan for tourism in Jamaica aims to develop more **eco-tourism** or *green tourism*, to protect the environment and preserve the way of life of local people.

Eco Lodge lies in an eighteen-acre tropical nature reserve resort with vast stretches of coastline. The area is undeveloped – there are no sprawling resorts and no huge hotels. The resort has cabins and camping for up to 30 people. Activities include:

- Meeting Jamaican families
- Spiritual and traditional music
- Prayer and meditation
- Massage and exercise
- Traditional meals, such as curried goat

**C** Eco Lodge in Jamaica

- Nature trails, boat trips and river gorge hiking
- Farm tour to see an orchid house and papaya farm
- Blue Mountain cycle tour.

# WHY DO TOURISTS COME BACK TO JAMAICA?

**Kingston** – Jamaica's capital city – here you can visit Rockfort, a seventeenth-century fortress, the Church of St Thomas and the eighteenth-century Headquarters House.

**Montego Bay Harbour Street market** – braiding and beading your hair and visiting the Rose Hall with its resident ghost are 'musts'.

**Ocho Rios** – the first tourist here was Christopher Columbus. Many more since have enjoyed the spectacular scenery. You can also enjoy the shopping, the food and the nightlife with its reggae music.

**The Blue Mountains**, which lie to the north of Kingston, appear blue when the mist hovers over them. Famous for their coffee-growing areas, they are also full of trails, rivers, waterfalls, birdlife and fruit.

**Negril**, at the far western tip, is famous for the fantastic sunsets and a seven-mile stretch of white beach.

**The South Coast** is largely untouched and is a wildlife haven for crocodiles and birds such as ostriches. There are also famous waterfalls and caves. Eco-tourism is being developed in this area (see **C**).

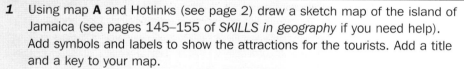

**D** The attractions of Jamaica

## Activities

1  Using map **A** and Hotlinks (see page 2) draw a sketch map of the island of Jamaica (see pages 145–155 of *SKILLS in geography* if you need help). Add symbols and labels to show the attractions for the tourists. Add a title and a key to your map.

2  a) Using **B**, draw a climate graph for Jamaica (see pages 145–155 of *SKILLS in geography*).

   b) Which would be the best month to visit Jamaica? Give reasons for your answer.

3  Use the information on these pages to answer this question: Is Jamaica a successful tourist destination?

   You need to think about the good and bad points of tourism for the country, its people and the tourists. Summarise your ideas in a poster on a large sheet of paper to share with the rest of the class. Add graphs and illustrations to help support your argument.

4  In pairs, look at the fact file on eco-tourism and use Hotlinks to look at the Eco Lodge website. In what ways is the Eco Lodge a good example of eco-tourism? In what ways may it be a poor example? Could anything be done to improve it?

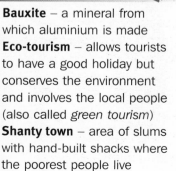

**Key words**

**Bauxite** – a mineral from which aluminium is made
**Eco-tourism** – allows tourists to have a good holiday but conserves the environment and involves the local people (also called *green tourism*)
**Shanty town** – area of slums with hand-built shacks where the poorest people live

# Managing tourism

## Key words

**Leakage** – when much of the money paid for a holiday goes to companies based in richer countries instead of the country visited

**Sustainable tourism** – tourism that does not damage the environment or the way of life of the local people

**Vicious cycle** – where one thing leads to another, which leads to another so that the situation gets worse and worse

Tourism has to be managed carefully. Countries like Jamaica earn a lot of money from tourism and it provides much-needed jobs, but there is a high level of **leakage** in tourism. This means that Jamaica gets very little of the money that tourists spend. It leaks out to all sorts of people and places. Look at what happens when a UK family books their package holiday to Jamaica.

- Some of the money goes direct to the travel agent.

- Some goes to the tour operator whose package they buy.

- Some goes to the airline, usually British.

- Some goes to the hotel-owners in America.

- A lot of the food and drink is also imported from abroad.

- The hotel manager and some of the other top staff are American, so their incomes are paid into bank accounts in their home country.

- Jamaicans are employed as waiters, cooks, cleaners, taxi drivers, etc. They earn very little and some are not employed all year round.

Imagine how much more money Jamaica could make from tourism if this leakage did not take place.

Tourism also brings with it conflicting viewpoints (see **A** and **B**).

'Been here nearly a week and haven't left the hotel – just relaxing! I'm avoiding the souvenir-sellers and their demands for money.'

'These rich tourists can be so greedy and rude – they make the beaches so crowded and make us short of water. They don't eat our home-grown food – it's all imported for them and we don't benefit at all. My friend works as a waiter and he sometimes earns less than me. They don't care about the people or the culture, or that most of their money goes to other countries.'

A

B

The chart in **C** shows what can happen if tourism is not carefully managed. This is often called a **vicious cycle**. Imagine the impact this would have on countries like Jamaica where the people are already poor and 45 per cent of their foreign income comes from tourism.

```
        Tour operators offer
        cheap packages
       ↗                    ↘
So prices have to be      More people book to
cut further               go because it is so
                          cheap
↑                              ↓
IN THE END NO ONE         So developers build
WANTS TO GO –             new hotels and
the industry declines     facilities
↑                              ↓
Now many tourists         But development is
are put off               not managed or
                          controlled
       ↖                    ↙
        So the resort's
        natural attractions
        are ruined
```

**C**  The vicious cycle of tourism – tourism can ruin a place

### How can we manage tourism?
Holidays are fun, and tourism can bring many benefits to the country that tourists visit and its people. But it can also do real harm: to the environment, to the people and to

their culture. Today many countries have a tourism development plan and they hope to make tourism more sustainable. But what does this mean? **Sustainable tourism** means that the tourist can still have a good time but without damaging the environment or the culture. The local people can also have a say in how the tourism is planned and earn a fair share of the profits that are made.

Sustainable tourism is important for all countries, both rich and poor, including the UK, Spain and Jamaica. It is especially important for the poor countries where the effect of a drop in tourism is much greater and where a thriving tourist industry can help millions of people have a better standard of living.

## How to be a sustainable tourist
Remember you are a guest in another person's country.

Get to know the people and their culture.

Dress and behave correctly – away from your resort, try to dress and behave like local people do.

Pack environmentally friendly products, e.g. shampoo, suntan lotion, cosmetics.

Support the local economy: buy local food, drinks, souvenirs and visit local attractions.

Stay in eco-friendly, locally owned accommodation.

Don't waste energy – have showers rather than baths, and switch off lights and air-conditioning when they aren't needed.

Don't waste water or drop litter.

Use public transport to visit places.

Ask permission before taking photographs.

## Activities

**1**  a) Look at the bulleted list on page 60. Can you think of any more ways money might leak away from Jamaica?

   b) In what ways do the local people benefit from tourism?

**2**  Look at photos **A** and **B** – in what other ways can tourism cause problems?

**3**  Look at **C**. It shows a possible vicious cycle. But countries like Jamaica can't afford to lose their tourist industry.

   a) If you were the Jamaican government, where would you step in? What would you do?

   b) Redraw the cycle to show how your actions would change the cycle for the better.

   c) Discuss your suggestions with a partner. Who had the best ideas? Why were they good?

**4**  Think about a holiday or day trip that you went on recently. Was it a package tour or was it more environmentally sustainable? Use the fact file to analyse your holiday. What did you do that was sustainable? What can you do to make your holidays more sustainable in the future?

# Tourism – good or bad?

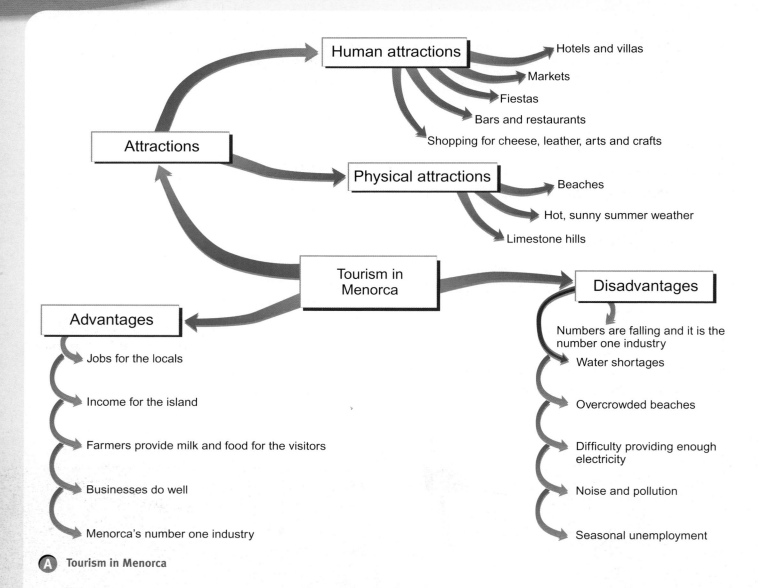

Human attractions
- Hotels and villas
- Markets
- Fiestas
- Bars and restaurants
- Shopping for cheese, leather, arts and crafts

Attractions

Physical attractions
- Beaches
- Hot, sunny summer weather
- Limestone hills

Tourism in Menorca

Advantages
- Jobs for the locals
- Income for the island
- Farmers provide milk and food for the visitors
- Businesses do well
- Menorca's number one industry

Disadvantages
- Numbers are falling and it is the number one industry
- Water shortages
- Overcrowded beaches
- Difficulty providing enough electricity
- Noise and pollution
- Seasonal unemployment

**A** Tourism in Menorca

*1* Use **A** as a base to draw a mental map for Jamaica or another holiday resort or country. Look at pages 145–155 of *SKILLS in geography* for help.

*2* Imagine you work for the Tourism Development Ministry in Menorca. In pairs or small groups, design and present a ten-point plan for the future development of tourism in Menorca. Use Hotlinks (see page 2) to find out about the historical attractions in Menorca. Could these be used in your plan to keep Menorcan tourism sustainable?

Write a brief summary at the end to explain the advantages of your plan. You could use ICT to do your presentation to the class. Remember to include a map and other images.

# >> 5    Rivers and floods

Have you seen waterfalls as large as these? These falls are in Brazil, one of the world's most water-rich countries. Can you think of any benefits and disadvantages of large rivers and waterfalls?

## *Learning objectives*

What are you going to learn about in this chapter?

> How the water cycle operates both above and below the ground
> The importance to people of both natural and human stores of fresh water
> River landforms in both upland and lowland areas
> Why rivers flood
> Whether or not people can prevent rivers from flooding
> How to investigate rivers using fieldwork

**A** Igacu Falls, on the border between Brazil and Argentina

# Water cycle – processes

> **Finding out how rivers fit into the water cycle**
> **Learning about how people use rivers**

The water cycle is complete when precipitation returns to the atmosphere as water vapour (page 34). It can be quick. Have you seen steam rising from roads after a summer thunderstorm? The steam shows the rainwater is evaporating immediately. On the other hand, it can take thousands (if not millions) of years if water is trapped in temporary stores on the surface or underground (see pages 66 and 67).

## PROCESSES

The main component processes of the water cycle are shown in **B**. Precipitation includes all types of moisture that reaches the Earth's surface from the atmosphere (see page 34). One type is shown in **A**. How many more can you name?

Once precipitation reaches the Earth's surface, one of the following three things happens to it.

**1** Return to the atmosphere by evaporation from water surfaces and by transpiration from plants. Evapo-transpiration is the name given to all losses of water from the surface into the atmosphere.

- High temperatures and strong winds increase the rate at which water droplets are changed into water vapour.

**2** Water movement over the surface as runoff, leading to the formation of rivers.

- Steep slopes, impermeable rocks and little vegetation cover increase the likelihood of runoff.

**A** Winter morning in the Lake District. Night cooling has led to condensation and precipitation. What shows this?

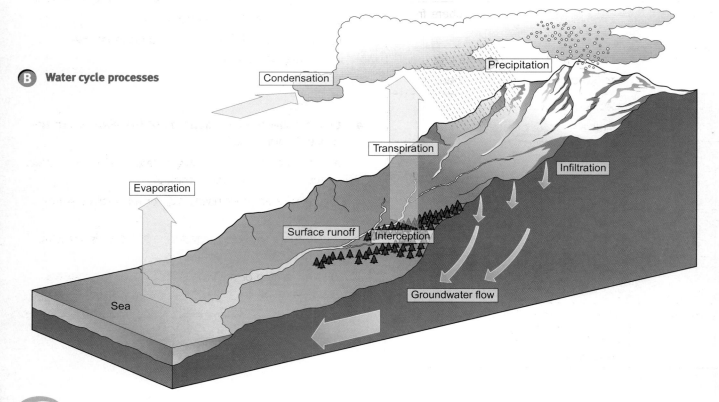

**B** Water cycle processes

Condensation

Precipitation

Transpiration

Infiltration

Evaporation

Surface runoff

Interception

Groundwater flow

Sea

- Woodland reduces runoff because the branches and leaves of trees intercept rain.

**3** Downward movement of water into the soil by infiltration.
- Where permeable rocks outcrop on the surface, water can infiltrate and move through the rock as groundwater flow.
- Light rain and gentle slopes help infiltration into the ground.

# RIVERS

Rivers are a vital part of the Earth's water cycle. They transfer rainwater from land to sea. Most rivers start in upland areas as very small streams; they gradually increase in size as other streams supply them with more water on the journey to the sea.

Access to a water supply was one of the main factors taken into account when choosing sites for settlements in the British Isles. Riverside locations are the most common sites for settlements because rivers are useful to people in many ways (**C**).

Bathing  Drinking  **Fishing**
Boating  water  Cooling water
Waste disposal  Canoeing
Irrigation water for crops  Ships and navigation
White water rafting
Hydro-electric power (HEP)
Swimming  Washing clothes
Water wheel  Water for making soft drinks and beer

**C**  Uses of rivers

## Activities

| Key words | Definition |
|---|---|
| Precipitation | downward movement of water into soil |
| Interception | loss of water from plants into the atmosphere |
| Runoff | rock with spaces and holes that allow water to pass through it |
| Infiltration | loss of water into the atmosphere from all surface sources |
| Permeable rock | water from lakes and seas is changed into water vapour, a gas, by heating |
| Groundwater flow | movement of water over the ground surface after precipitation |
| Evaporation | water vapour, a gas, is changed into water as a liquid in water droplets and clouds by cooling |
| Transpiration | when rain is prevented from reaching the ground by trees |
| Evapo-transpiration | movement of water through spaces and holes in rock |
| Condensation | all forms of moisture that reach the ground surface, e.g. snow, rain, sleet, dew |

**1** **Key words – mix and match**

First copy the list of key words. Then write the correct definition next to each key word.

**2** Look at **A**.

a) Name *one* type of precipitation shown.

b) Can you think why it often occurs on winter mornings in the UK?

**3** Rearrange the uses of rivers in **C** under these headings.

a) Water supply for domestic purposes

b) Water supply for industrial and business use

c) Leisure and recreation

d) Transport

e) Energy

**4** **Group activity – Investigation of the river or stream nearest your school**

a) Find out basic details, e.g. where it starts and ends, which places it passes through.

b) Describe its main uses, e.g. for recreation, water supply.

c) Are there any disadvantages, e.g. for roads crossing over it, dumping waste?

d) Draw a map or sketches to show how the river and land around it are used.

e) Make an overall judgement – is the river an asset or a problem?

# Water cycle – stores and water supply

> **Learning about water stores**
> **Finding out about water as a natural resource**

Water is a **natural resource**. Fresh water is *the most valuable* of all the Earth's natural resources, because human life on Earth would be impossible without it.

## FACT FILE  WHAT IS A WATER STORE?

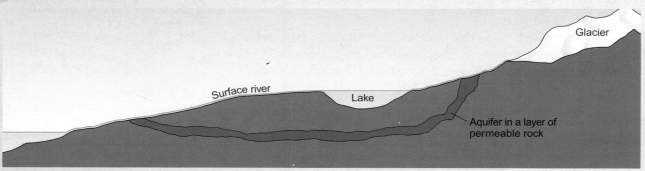

**A**  Natural stores of fresh water

These are points in the water cycle where water movement is held up or stored for a time before being allowed to continue. Natural stores on land are shown in **A**. In which one of them is the largest amount of fresh water on Earth stored? You can find the answer in **B**.

Natural stores of fresh water are important sources of human water supply, but they are not evenly distributed over the Earth's surface and not always found in areas where most people live. Only 13 per cent of water on Earth is fresh water; of this, more than half is stored in Antarctica – the only continent without permanent settlement. Water locked up in ice is not available for use by people until it melts. To increase water supplies, rivers are dammed and **reservoirs** are built.

### Where does it come from?
Do you know where in the UK the water that flows from your taps at home comes from? If you live north and west of the Tees–Exe line it will probably come from mountain lakes or upland reservoirs filled by rivers. If you live in East Anglia and South East England there is a higher chance that your water supply will come from **aquifers** – underground stores in permeable rocks, especially chalk. A check for limescale on the inside of your electric kettle will soon tell you whether or not your domestic water supply comes from areas of chalk or limestone. Water is also drawn directly from large rivers such as the Thames without previous storage. Look at **C**. Has this water already been used in towns upstream and recycled? Will it be used again in London?

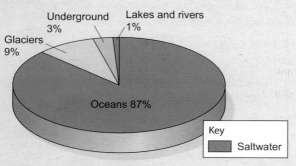

**B**  Water stores on the Earth's surface

Glaciers 9%
Underground 3%
Lakes and rivers 1%
Oceans 87%

Key
Saltwater

**C**  Summer users of the River Thames at Reading

The UK has many rivers. Most people will readily agree that the UK has a wet climate. Despite this, the UK is not 'water-rich' by world standards (see **D**). This is because the UK has a high population density. Even 'dry' Australia (with its image of being all outback and desert) is fifteen times better off for water per head than the UK.

Another big problem for water supply in the UK is that the greatest concentration of people is in London and the South East where rainfall is lowest. Also this is where the government is planning future housing increases.

|  | Water per head (m³) |
|---|---|
| UK | 1 219 |
| World average | 6 918 |
| Europe average | 8 547 |
| Australia | 18 596 |

 **Water resources**

# London 'could be without water inside ten years'

*L*ondon could run out of water within a decade if it does not spend more on replacing leaking mains built in Victorian times or on building reservoirs, Thames Water said yesterday.

The company has warned that the population of London is now expected to grow by 800 000 by 2016. Demand for water will be greater than existing supplies. Population growth and new housing will place severe pressure on the capital's water supplies.

Thames Water has already announced its intention to build a desalination plant (to extract fresh water from sea water) within three years to provide drinking water for 900 000 people.

Dry summers already cause problems for the company. 'We have nothing up our sleeves to keep things running in a dry summer,' said the managing director.

 Adapted from a newspaper report by Charlie Clover, Environment editor, *Daily Telegraph,* **23 October 2004.** © Telegraph Group Limited (2004)

## Activities

**1** a) Draw a labelled diagram to show the natural stores of water.

   b) The order of importance for human water supply in the world is:

   1 Surface rivers   2 Underground aquifers   3 Lakes   4 Glaciers

   (i)  Why do you think rivers are the most important?

   (ii) Choose *one* of the others and explain why it is less important.

**2** Draw a bar graph to show the values in table **D**.

**3** a) State *two* reasons why water supply is a greater problem in London and the South East than in other parts of the UK.

   b) Describe how Thames Water is hoping to reduce the problem.

   c) Can they solve the problem or just reduce it? Explain what you think.

**4** a) Find out the name of the Water Authority that provides water in your home region.

   b) Visit its website to discover where your tap water comes from.

   c) Is water supply plentiful in your region, even in a drought? Look at the evidence on these pages and explain.

**Key words**

**Aquifer** – underground store of water in permeable rock
**Natural resource** – something that occurs naturally that people can use
**Reservoir** – artificial lake used to store water for human use

# Rivers in the uplands

> **Understanding the work of rivers in the uplands**
> **Finding out about the common upland river landforms**

Each river has its own **drainage basin** (see **A**). The **source** is where the river starts in the uplands. The **mouth** is where it meets the sea. Between the two, the main river is fed by smaller rivers and rivers called **tributaries** that increase its size.

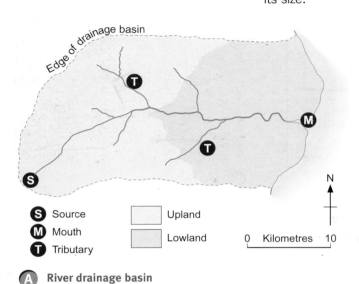

**S** Source
**M** Mouth
**T** Tributary

Upland
Lowland

0 Kilometres 10

N

**A** River drainage basin

**B** River Tees in its upper course: notice the rocky bed and steep gradient typical of a river in the uplands

## FACT FILE — THE WORK OF RIVERS IN THE UPLANDS

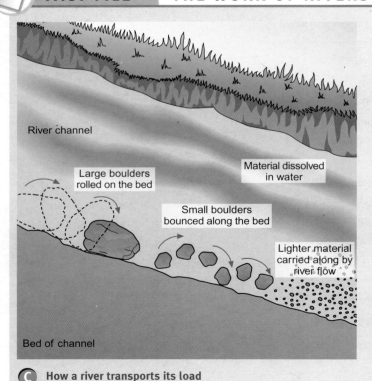

River channel

Large boulders rolled on the bed

Small boulders bounced along the bed

Material dissolved in water

Lighter material carried along by river flow

Bed of channel

When a river has spare energy, it does two types of work.

1 It transports boulders, stones, and fine material such as sand and silt. The total amount carried by a river is its **load**. Ways of transporting this load vary with the types of materials being transported (see **C**).

2 It erodes the bed and banks of its **channel**. It does this in several different ways, but the two most important ones are *abrasion and hydraulic action* (see **D**), just as they were for wave erosion.

### Abrasion
Boulders, bounced along the bed, break off pieces of rock as they are moved.

### Hydraulic action
Water washes against the bed and banks, dislodges and removes materials.

**C** How a river transports its load

**D** How rivers erode

# UPLAND RIVER LANDFORMS

Rivers form **V-shaped valleys** (**E** and **F**). Why? The channel bed is always the lowest part of a valley; this is where bed and banks are being eroded by moving water. Rivers in the uplands are flowing high above sea level; they cut downwards into the rock, which is called **vertical erosion**. Sometimes the valley sides are so high, steep and rocky that they form a **gorge**.

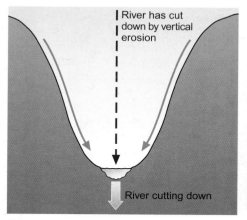

River has cut down by vertical erosion

River cutting down

**E** How a V-shaped valley and gorge are formed

**F** V-shaped valley

**G** Gorge

The river landform in upland areas that attracts most visitors is the **waterfall**, where water cascades over a large vertical drop. The three things to look for when studying a waterfall are:

- hard rock at the top (called the *cap rock*) – this is eroded only slowly
- soft rocks below – these are easier to erode, leaving the hard rock overhanging
- plunge pool at the bottom – formed by the force of the falling water.

## Activities

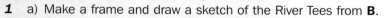

**1** a) Make a frame and draw a sketch of the River Tees from **B**.

b) Add labels to show the features of a river in the uplands.

c) Now compare your sketch with those of people near you in the class. Mark your neighbour's sketch out of ten using this guide to marking:

- Amount of detail shown – up to four marks
- Appearance and neatness – up to two marks
- Number of labels used – up to four marks.

d) What have others in the class done better? How could your own sketch have been improved?

**2** Look at **E–G**.

a) Draw sketch cross-sections to show the difference between a steep-sided V-shaped valley and a gorge.

b) Describe *two* features that make a gorge attractive to visitors.

**3** Draw and label a storyboard for an animation to show your class how a river transports its load.

### Key words

**Channel** – area between the banks where the river flows

**Drainage basin** – area of land drained by a river and its tributaries

**Gorge** – deep, narrow, steep-sided valley

**Load** – all materials transported by a river

**Mouth** – point where a river goes into the sea

**Source** – point where a river starts to flow

**Tributary** – smaller river that flows into a larger one

**Vertical erosion** – wearing away land in a downward direction

**V-shaped valley** – river valley that is lowest in the centre

**Waterfall** – where the river suddenly drops in height

# Rivers in the lowlands

> Understanding the work of rivers in the lowlands
> Finding out about the common lowland river landforms

Several changes in the channel and valley can be noticed when a river leaves the uplands (see photos **A** and **B**).

- The channel becomes wider and deeper.
- There are fewer boulders in the channel bed, and water flow is smoother.
- Bends in the river are more pronounced.
- The sides of the V-shaped valley become less steep.

**A** River on the edge of the Pennine uplands

**B** River Cuckmere in Sussex, almost at the sea

## FACT FILE  HOW IS THE WORK OF RIVERS DIFFERENT IN THE LOWLANDS?

There are two main differences from rivers in the uplands.

1 The river wears away land on the *sides* of the channel and on valley *sides*, which is called **lateral erosion**.

2 Deposition is an important process as the river drops most of the sediment it was transporting.

Together these processes have a great effect upon landforms (see **C**). Lateral erosion is responsible for the large bends in river channels that lead to the formation of **meanders** and **ox-bow lakes**. Deposition creates raised banks, known as **levees**, and leads to the formation of the flat **floodplains**, built mainly of **silt**.

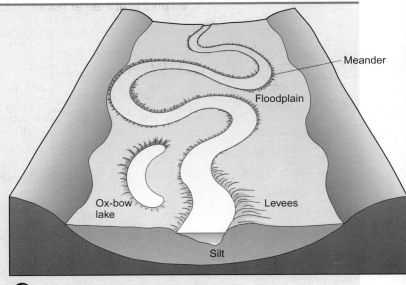

**C** River landforms in the lowlands

# LOWLAND RIVER LANDFORMS

Studying the formation of meanders and ox-bow lakes is useful because it shows how rivers both erode on the sides and deposit (see **D**).

- On a bend the main river current swings towards the outside bend.
- The bank on the outside bend is eroded and forms a steep bank.
- On the inside bend water flow is slow.
- Sediment is deposited here to form a gentle bank.
- During a flood the river breaks through the narrow neck between two outside bends and forms an ox-bow lake.

Rivers in flood look brown because they carry large loads of sediment. Every time a river floods it leaves a new layer of sediment behind; over time, this builds up into a great thickness of silt and forms a floodplain. In a flood, more silt is deposited on the banks next to the river than further away; over time, this builds up levees. Floodplains are widened by lateral erosion on the outside bends of meanders.

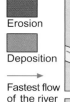
Erosion

Deposition

Fastest flow of the river

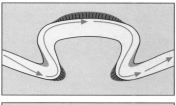
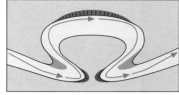
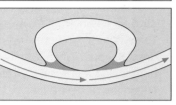

**D** Formation of a meander and an ox-bow lake

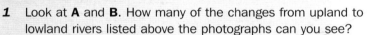
## Activities  (S) 📄 (A)

**1**  Look at **A** and **B**. How many of the changes from upland to lowland rivers listed above the photographs can you see?

**2**  a) Make a frame and draw a grid the same size as the OS map in **E**.

   b) On your map: show the course of the River Nidd; shade and name the *two* largest settlements and draw the line of the 20 m contour.

   c) Write X in a likely place for an ox-bow lake to form in the future. Explain why you wrote X in that place.

   d) Which of the two settlements is at greater risk of flooding? Explain your answer.

**3**  **Odd one out**

| | | |
|---|---|---|
| 1 Abrasion | 6 Levees | 11 Silt |
| 2 Channel | 7 Meander | 12 Source |
| 3 Floodplain | 8 Mouth | 13 Vertical erosion |
| 4 Gorge | 9 Ox-bow lake | 14 V-shaped valley |
| 5 Lateral erosion | 10 Plunge pool | 15 Waterfall |

   a) For each set below, decide which is the odd one out. Give a reason for your choice.

   **Set A:**  1  5  11  13    **Set B:**  4  6  10  15

   b) Make *two* sets of your own. Test them on your neighbour.

**E**  OS map of part of the valley of the River Nidd between Knaresborough and York, scale 1:50 000.

© Crown copyright, Licence no. 100000230

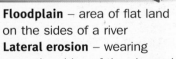

### Key words

**Floodplain** – area of flat land on the sides of a river

**Lateral erosion** – wearing away the sides of the channel and valley

**Levees** – raised banks on the side of a river forming a natural embankment

**Meander** – large bend in the river

**Ox-bow lake** – semi-circular lake on the side of a river

**Silt** – fine-grained sediment carried and deposited by rivers

# Why do rivers flood?

> Understanding the causes of flooding
> Finding out what happens to the excess water/runoff in urban and rural surfaces

## FACT FILE  WHEN DO FLOODS HAPPEN?

Flooding occurs when too much water reaches a river channel; water flows over the top of the banks onto the land beyond. It is normal for rivers to flood several times a year. Three natural landforms on pages 70 and 71 are formed by rivers in flood. Which are they? Of course, for people with homes and businesses located on or near river floodplains, floods are at best a nuisance and at worst a danger to life and a great economic cost.

**A**  River Ouse in flood at York, one of the most flood-prone cities in the UK

### Natural causes of flooding

It is possible to identify three natural causes of flooding.

1 Persistent rain day after day

Small daily totals can add up to a large amount if it rains every day for a week. The ground becomes saturated so that no more rainwater can be absorbed by soil and rocks. All the rest of the rain is surface runoff into rivers.

2 Heavy rain, as in a thunderstorm

Water droplets hit the ground with such force that there is little chance of seepage into the ground (see **C**).

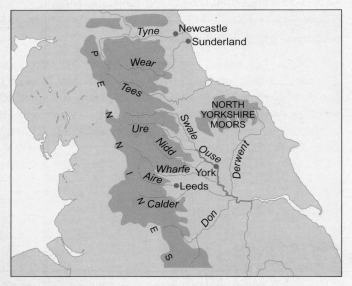

**B**  The main rivers in northern and eastern England. Why does the River Ouse flood more than any of the other rivers?

3 Melting snow and ice

Rivers that begin in high mountain areas, like those in the Alps, usually flood in summer when temperatures are high enough to melt the ice and snow on the mountain tops.

**C**  One cause of flooding – a cloudburst

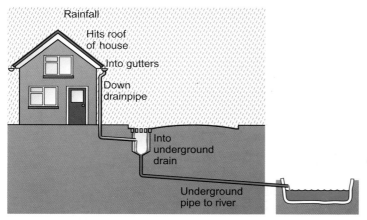

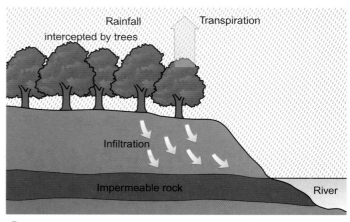

**D** Water movement in built-up urban areas

**E** Water movement on vegetation-covered surfaces

# HOW PEOPLE INCREASE THE RISK OF FLOODING

Humans change the ways in which land is used – often without any thought for likely consequences for runoff. Look what happens in built-up areas (**D**). Rainwater falling on paved surfaces and roofs of buildings is led rapidly into underground drains, with little chance of evaporation or infiltration into the ground.

Compare this with what happens in rural areas on surfaces covered by vegetation (**E**). Rainwater stays on the ground for as long as possible, increasing the opportunities for evapo-transpiration and infiltration into the ground. After all, water is vital for plant growth.

Flooding is only a problem when it directly affects people. This problem is increasing all the time as population increases and more building takes place on floodplains. In the UK, the number of properties at risk from flooding rose to 2.2 million by 2004, an increase of 300 000 since 2001. The same is happening in many other areas throughout the world as well.

|  | Forest | Built-up |
|---|---|---|
| Evapo-transpiration | 40% | 25% |
| Runoff | 10% | 45% |
| Groundwater | 50% | 30% |

**F** What happens to precipitation (100%) in woodland and city areas

## Activities

**1** a) Draw a labelled diagram to show what a river in flood looks like.

   b) State as many bad points about river floods as you can.

**2** a) The River Ouse from York southwards floods more often than any of the other rivers named in **B**. Can you explain why?

   b) What do you think 'Sunwac' stands for? Look at **B** and suggest what this mnenomic is helping people to remember.

**3** a) Look at **F**. Draw *two* pie graphs side by side to show these percentages. Look at *SKILLS in geography* pages 145–155 for help.

   b) Look at **D** and **E**. With the help of diagrams, explain in more detail why flooding is more likely in cities.

**4** Visit the Environment Agency's website via Hotlinks (see page 2). Enter your postcode to check your area for flood risk to your school and home.
Suggest reasons for the level of risk shown.

# The Boscastle flood in August 2004

> Finding out how flooding affects people in the UK
> Practising interpreting evidence from an OS map

## FACT FILE — LYNMOUTH FLOOD IN AUGUST 1952

The short steep-sided valleys of North Devon and North Cornwall are particularly vulnerable to flooding after localised summer downpours. Perhaps the most famous flood in the UK happened in the North Devon fishing village of Lynmouth in 1952.

**First two weeks of August**
Weather much wetter than usual; ground saturated.

**15 August**
Rain for 24 hours during which 270 mm fell on Exmoor.

**Night of 15–16 August**
- Wave of water 4 m high burst into the village at 300 kph (200 mph).

- It carried boulders, trees and telegraph poles.
- Debris collected against bridges, forming dams.
- When these burst, surges of water 10 m high were released.

**Morning of 16 August**
- In all, 35 people were killed.
- One-quarter of the built-up area was devastated.
- Twenty-eight homes were washed away, sixteen bridges destroyed, 100 vehicles swept out to sea and nineteen boats missing.

## BOSCASTLE FLOOD IN 2004

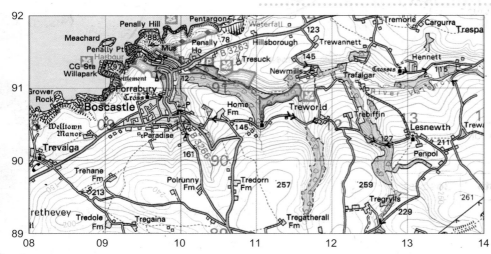

 **A** OS map of Boscastle, scale 1:50 000.
© Crown copyright, Licence no. 100000230

History almost repeated itself when a summer storm centred over the moors three or four miles east of Boscastle (**A**) dropped 200 mm of rain, most of it within four hours during the middle of the day. In the wettest hour 90 mm fell, with an intensity that is rarely witnessed outside the tropics. It poured down the steep hillsides into the rivers Valencey and Jordan, which meet in Boscastle, and produced a genuine *flash flood* – when river flow responds *instantly* to a cloudburst (**B**).

The three-metre high wall of water that swept through the village washed 30 vehicles into the harbour. It uprooted trees and piled them up next to houses and behind the bridges. Two shops on the riverside were destroyed, other properties were badly damaged and one bridge collapsed. More than 100 people were plucked to safety by helicopters from roofs and trees. It was a miracle that no one died; this was largely thanks to the people in the emergency services, who responded with speed and efficiency. The fact that it happened in the middle of the day also helped.

**83-year-old local man:**
'I have never seen it rain as hard as this in all my life.'

**House owner:**
'It was a normal summer morning, quite peaceful really. In the early afternoon it suddenly turned into a place of mayhem, as water waist-deep swept cars away past our front door. We had to punch holes in the roof of our house to escape the water and await rescue by helicopter.'

**Hotel guest:**
'One minute the water was ankle-deep. The next minute the water was up to our chests. We ran up the stairs. The water just rose up after us. It was like a horror film.'

**Local councillor:**
'I do not think anything could have been built to hold back this kind of rainfall.'

**Tourist:**
'When the waters started to rise in the river bed, at first it was more like a tourist attraction. The car park was full of people looking at the water. Then the river banks suddenly burst and people started fleeing for their lives.'

**Local resident:**
'The rain turned the roads into rivers. Cars, wheelie bins and trees went flying past in a torrent of water and disappeared out to sea.'

**B** Floodwater sweeps through the centre of Boscastle

**C** Comments from witnesses of the flood

## Activities

1. Make a large summary chart like the one below for the Lynmouth and Boscastle floods.

| | Lynmouth | Boscastle |
|---|---|---|
| Time of year | | |
| Weather | | |
| What the flood was like | | |
| Numbers killed | | |
| Damage to property | | |

2. State what you consider to be the *three* main similarities between the Lynmouth and Boscastle floods.

3. Which one of the two floods was the more serious? Explain your choice.

4. Write a newspaper report (300–400 words) that a reporter could have written, looking at the scene in **B** and talking to the people in **C**.

5. Study OS map **A**.

   a) Describe the physical features of the drainage basin of the River Valencey (e.g. what the valley sides are like, number of tributaries, etc.).

   b) Why is it the type of drainage basin that produces rapid runoff in heavy rain?

   c) State reasons why only that part of Boscastle sited in square 0991 was flooded.

   d) Describe the map evidence for many visitors to this area.

   e) The flood caused traffic chaos on the B3263 road. Why? How many reasons can you think of for this?

# Flood prevention measures

> Finding out what can be done to prevent floods
> Discovering the advantages and disadvantages of human intervention

Some of the most commonly used ways to try to prevent river flooding are shown in **A**. The amount done increases from left to right – so also does the cost.

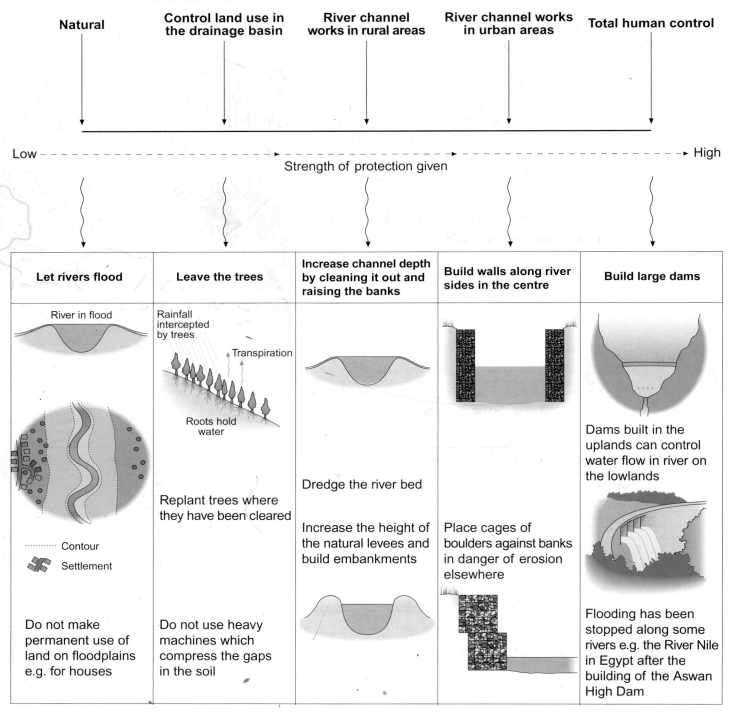

| Natural | Control land use in the drainage basin | River channel works in rural areas | River channel works in urban areas | Total human control |
|---|---|---|---|---|

Low - - - - - - - - - - - - - - - - - - - - - - - - - - - - - - - - - - - - - - - - - - - - - - → High

Strength of protection given

| **Let rivers flood** | **Leave the trees** | **Increase channel depth by cleaning it out and raising the banks** | **Build walls along river sides in the centre** | **Build large dams** |
|---|---|---|---|---|
| River in flood | Rainfall intercepted by trees | | | |
| | Transpiration | | | |
| | Roots hold water | | | Dams built in the uplands can control water flow in river on the lowlands |
| Contour / Settlement | Replant trees where they have been cleared | Dredge the river bed | Place cages of boulders against banks in danger of erosion elsewhere | |
| Do not make permanent use of land on floodplains e.g. for houses | Do not use heavy machines which compress the gaps in the soil | Increase the height of the natural levees and build embankments | | Flooding has been stopped along some rivers e.g. the River Nile in Egypt after the building of the Aswan High Dam |

 **Different measures to prevent flooding**

# ADVANTAGES AND DISADVANTAGES OF DIFFERENT MEASURES

In rural areas flood prevention measures are usually small-scale. Any damage they cause to the local environment is only slight. They are not intended to stop river flooding entirely but to reduce the number of floods and their severity. Most channel works in rural areas are done to benefit local farming communities.

However, in urban areas channel works are essential. There are more people and property to protect. Walled banks are common along the sides of rivers through towns and cities, but are often not enough by themselves to stop large rivers from flooding during extreme weather (**B**). In places with a high flood risk metal gates can be closed after flood warnings to protect riverside properties (**C**).

The most complete method of flood control is building a large dam. In times of heavy rainfall the dam holds back all the runoff; when river levels return to normal, water from behind the dam can be released gradually. Large dams have other uses: domestic water supply, irrigation and electricity generation. Unfortunately, they come with large costs:

- money – very expensive to build
- human – people are forced to move from the valley to be flooded
- environmental – flooding leads to loss of wildlife habitats.

**B** The River Wear in Durham in flood for the second time in the wet year of 2000

**C** High walls and metal gates protect housing on the banks of the River Tees in Yarm

## Activities

**1** Make a large chart to show *four* measures of flood prevention, their advantages and disadvantages. Some ideas about what to do are given below.

| Measure of flood prevention | Where used? | Advantages | Disadvantages |
|---|---|---|---|
| **1** Making the embankments higher<br>*Insert sketch here, label main features* | *Countryside or town?*<br>*Big river or small?* | *Benefits for people, e.g. farmers, businesses, householders* | *Its costs for people and the environment* |
| **2** | | | |

**2** Investigate the river flowing through your nearest town or city.

   a) Name and describe the measures of flood prevention in use along the river.

   b) How large an area do they cover?

   c) Have they been 100 per cent effective so far?

# Investigating rivers using fieldwork

> Learning about safety precautions during river fieldwork
> Finding out what can be investigated in river fieldwork and how to do it

Doing river fieldwork can be great fun. It is a great chance to work in a group with your friends. It is impossible to work alone because you need others to help with holding the equipment, taking the measurements and noting the results down on a recording sheet. Is the river in **A** of a suitable size for ease and safety of doing river fieldwork?

Doing river fieldwork can also be dangerous and it is important to think about safety (see **B**). Deep pools, strong currents and rapid variations in water level are possible safety hazards. Choose a river or stream of manageable width and depth like the one in **A**. Never do fieldwork in rivers when thunderstorms are forecast. Why?

(A) Group of geography students investigating a river

(B) Safety first

## FACT FILE    PLANNING A FIELDWORK INVESTIGATION OF A RIVER

**1 Find a title.**

Ask yourself: 'What do I want to find out?' One common title for a river study is:

 *'In what ways and why does the channel of River ... change downstream?'*

The most likely changes downstream in a river and its channel will be:

- they will get wider and deeper (because the river is joined by more tributaries)

- water speed will increase (because a larger river can flow more smoothly)

- load size will decrease (because boulders and pebbles are replaced by small stones and sand).

**2 Prepare to do the fieldwork.**

- Draw a recording sheet (your teacher can give you an example to help).

- Assemble the measuring equipment.

Then you should be ready to start.

# WHAT CAN BE INVESTIGATED AND HOW?

Channel width and depth, speed of river flow and load size are basic measurements taken in most river studies (see **C**).

**Channel width** is measured at the water surface using a tape measure or long rope.

**Channel depth** is measured using a metric rule at intervals evenly spaced across the stream.

**Surface speed** can be measured with a flow metre. Not everyone has access to one of these, which is why the method below is used more often. It is also more interesting.

- Measure a 10 metre stretch of river.
- Throw a float into the river at the start. Possible floats include pieces of wood, oranges, onions and dog biscuits.
- Use a stopwatch to time how long it takes the float to go 10 metres.
- Calculate surface speed using this formula:

$$\text{Surface speed} = \frac{\text{Distance}}{\text{Time}}$$

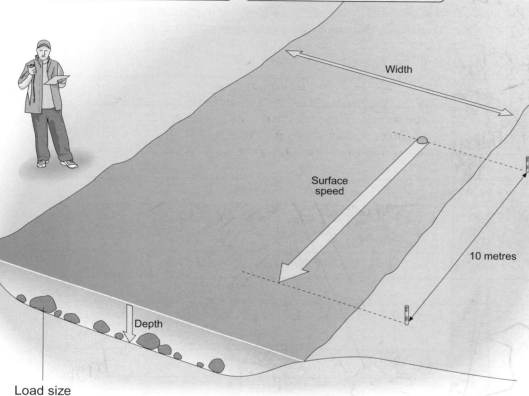

Width

Surface speed

Depth

10 metres

Load size

**C** Measurements that can be taken along a river

**Load size** is obtained by measuring pebbles and stones from the stream bed using a ruler. Take a sample of up to ten pebbles from the river bed, measure the longest edges and calculate the average length of pebbles in your sample.

## Activities

1. Make a list of the equipment needed for undertaking river fieldwork of the type described here.

2. Is the river in **A** of a suitable size for fieldwork? Explain.

3. Think of reasons for each of the following.

   a) Float measurements for river speed should be made more than once at each site.

   b) Up to ten pebbles or stones should be measured at each site for load size.

   c) Observations are made of the river valley as well.

4. Look back at earlier pages in this chapter. As a river travels from source to mouth, describe the changes expected in a) the river channel and b) landforms in the river and its valley.

# How can the results from river fieldwork be used?

> **Interpreting river fieldwork**

A group of students carried out an investigation titled: 'How does the river change between its source and the village of Langley?' The group studied a total of six sites; you can see channel depth and width measurements for three of the sites in **A**.

| | | | | | | | | | | | | | | | | |
|---|---|---|---|---|---|---|---|---|---|---|---|---|---|---|---|---|
| **Site 1** | **Location:** Close to source of stream | | | | | | | | | | **Width:** 1.7 m | | | | | |
| | **Depth** (metres from bank) | 0.5 | 1.0 | 1.5 | ~ | ~ | ~ | ~ | ~ | ~ | ~ | ~ | ~ | ~ | ~ | ~ |
| | depth (cm) | 7 | 10 | 4 | | | | | | | | | | | | |
| | **Valley observation:** Small and narrow | | | | | | | | | | | | | | | |
| **Site 3** | **Location:** Below the road bridge | | | | | | | | | | **Width:** 5.2 m | | | | | |
| | **Depth** (metres from bank) | 0.5 | 1.0 | 1.5 | 2.0 | 2.5 | 3.0 | 3.5 | 4.0 | 4.5 | 5.0 | ~ | ~ | ~ | ~ | |
| | depth (cm) | 10 | 10 | 11 | 12 | 14 | 15 | 15 | 13 | 12 | 10 | | | | | |
| | **Valley observation:** Flat land near the river, rising ground further away from river | | | | | | | | | | | | | | | |
| **Site 6** | **Location:** Next to the village | | | | | | | | | | **Width:** 7.1 m | | | | | |
| | **Depth** (metres from bank) | 0.5 | 1.0 | 1.5 | 2.0 | 2.5 | 3.0 | 3.5 | 4.0 | 4.5 | 5.0 | 5.5 | 6.0 | 6.5 | 7.0 | |
| | depth (cm) | 6 | 7 | 7 | 8 | 8 | 8 | 10 | 15 | 17 | 20 | 19 | 19 | 18 | 14 | |
| | **Valley observation:** Floodplain on both sides of the river | | | | | | | | | | | | | | | |

**A** Examples from a recording sheet for river fieldwork at three study sites

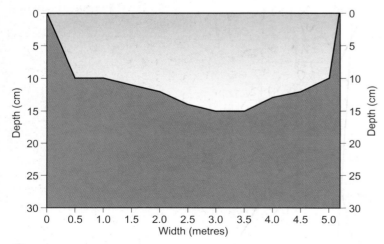

**B** Channel cross-section at site 3

It is not always easy to understand data about river depth on a recording sheet or in a table. It is difficult to imagine what this river is really like. This is why geographers use a lot of graphs, photographs and sketches when writing about fieldwork results.

### Site 3 as an example

Once width and depth have been measured, it is possible to draw a channel cross-section (**B**). This makes it a lot easier to see what the river channel was really like. It shows that the depth was similar across the river, just slightly deeper in the middle. This is the cross-section shape associated with a straight section of river. This is confirmed by looking at a photograph of site 3 in **C**. In **D** you can see what one of the students wrote about site 3.

Photograph taken at study site 3

## Activities

(S)

1  From the student's write-up in **D**, write down examples of where the student is:

   a) describing what the cross-section shows

   b) explaining how the river has changed and why it is different from earlier sites.

2  Photographs used in fieldwork write-ups should always be labelled.

   a) Make a large frame and draw a sketch of what can be seen in **C**.

   b) Add labels to show some of the channel and valley features that the student refers to in the write-up.

3  a) Using the values in **A**, draw channel cross-sections for sites 1 and 6.

   b) Describe what each cross-section shows.

4  The title for this fieldwork was: 'How does the river change between its source and the village of Langley?' You are going to use the fieldwork results to answer these questions.

   a) Describe the main differences in river channel and valley between sites 1 and 6.

   b) Give reasons for the main changes.

5  From what you have learned about rivers in this chapter, would you say that this is a typical river? Explain your answer.

The river channel is now three times wider than it was at the source. It is also deeper. The water in the channel is more than 10 cm deep and deeper still in the middle: up to 15 cm deep. The river is wider and deeper now because two tributaries have joined it.

There are some large stones on the river bed. They are causing ripples as the river flows over them. These can be seen on the photograph. The photograph also shows that the banks of the channel are quite steep and deep. I think that the river must still be cutting downwards by vertical erosion. All of these are features of a river in the uplands.

There is one big difference from site 1. Land beyond the river banks is now flatter. It seems to me that a floodplain is starting to form. You can also see this on the photograph. The land around the river is now lower and flatter than it was.

(D) Student's write-up for site 3

# Can river flooding in the UK be stopped?

**A  University lecturer in geography**
'Don't people understand why the flat land next to rivers is called the floodplain? River flooding is a natural event – all rivers flood. You could say that it is their own fault if people are having problems with flooding.'

**B  Director of a house-building company**
'Building new houses on flat land is easier than building on slopes. Buying floodplain land off farmers is cheap, because it is only useful for summer pasture. We are making better use of the land.'

**C  House owner**
'We looked around the house on a beautiful summer's day and fell in love with it. It cost us over £200 000. We put all our savings into it and still needed a big mortgage. Last winter the local stream flooded us out, twice. What is our dream house worth now? '

**D  Shop owner in the flood zone**
'I blame the Council for not keeping up with river works to stop these floods. How are they spending all the money I pay them in business rates?'

**E  Council leader**
'The number and size of river floods seem to be increasing because of global warming. With more government money, new protection measures could be built. But even with more government money, I do not think we can remove the risk of flooding altogether.'

**A** Some views on flooding

1  Who thinks that river flooding can be stopped?
  a) Draw a line like the one below, showing the two extreme views.

| Impossible to stop | Can be stopped by spending money |
|---|---|

  b) Read the views of the five people in **A**. Put the letters A to E where you think they should go along this line.
  c) (i)  What is your own view about stopping river floods? Mark M on the line for 'my own view'.
     (ii)  Explain why you placed M on the line where you did.
2  Write a page about: 'Why different people have different views about river flooding and how to stop it'. Think about the reasons for their views.

# >> 6   Italy

**Would you like to live somewhere like this? This is the hilltop settlement of Rivello in the south of Italy. What are the difficulties of living on the top of a hill? How is the landscape different from landscapes in the UK?**

## *Learning objectives*

What are you going to learn about in this chapter?

> The major features of the physical and human geography of Italy

> How Italy can be divided into a rich North and less wealthy South

> Why the gap in wealth between North and South opened up and why it is difficult to close

> Why Italy is an attractive destination for many different types of tourists

> How Venice is unique and why this causes big problems

> Italy's ageing population and why it is about to cause a pensions crisis

 Rivello, Italy

# Physical background

> **Understanding the physical geography of Italy**
> **Learning about Italy's climate**

**A** Physical map of Italy

**Key**
- Land over 1000 m
- Land between 500 and 1000 m
- Land under 500 m
- Lake
- • Major city
- ▲ Volcano

The easiest country to recognise on a map of Europe must be Italy. Shaped like a boot, and almost treating Sicily like a football, it forms a peninsula of land extending a long way into the Mediterranean Sea. The country consists of the mainland and a number of Mediterranean islands, the two largest of which are Sicily and Sardinia (map **A**).

## DIVIDING ITALY INTO PHYSICAL REGIONS

A physical **region** is an area with one or more features that are the same. Where are the boundaries between regions drawn? It depends upon the feature chosen and how much detail is needed. Look at map **A**. How many different physical regions can you see? Some possibilities are listed in **C**.

The feature that decides the choice of these regions is relief. The Alps form a towering mountain range. The highest mountain peaks in Europe straddle the borders between Italy and its Alpine neighbours – France, Switzerland and Austria. The jagged mountain peaks are topped by snow and ice. Large lakes fill the floors of deep, steep-sided mountain valleys.

Although the Apennines form a mountainous backbone that runs almost the full length of the peninsula, they are lower than the Alps (all peaks are below 3000 metres). The landscape is rugged with many outcrops of bare limestone rock, particularly in the south (photo **B**). In the north, there are many rolling hills covered by forest, green fields and vineyards. The highest mountain in the south is not in the Apennines; it is Mount Etna, the active volcano that dominates the geography of eastern Sicily.

**B** Apennines in southern Italy

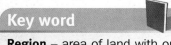

**Key word**

**Region** – area of land with one or more similar features

| Two regions | Three regions | Four regions |
|---|---|---|
| 1  Mountains | 1  Alps | 1  Alps |
| 2  Lowlands | 2  North Italian Plain | 2  North Italian Plain |
|  | 3  Peninsular Italy and islands | 3  Apennines |
|  |  | 4  Islands |

**C** How can Italy be divided into physical regions?

In a mountainous and hilly country like Italy (see table **D**) the lowlands on the sides of the River Po which make up the North Italian Plain stand out as being very different from the rest of the country. The River Po, Italy's longest river, is supplied with water from many Alpine rivers. It flows across a wide floodplain where typical river landforms such as meanders and levees are common. It forms the largest area of flat land in Italy.

| Region | Area (millions of hectares) |
|---|---|
| Italy (total) | 30.1 |
| Mountain (above 700 m) | 10.6 |
| Hill (150 m to 700 m) | 12.5 |
| Lowland and plain (below 150 m) | 7.0 |

**D** Italy – summary of relief

## CLIMATES OF ITALY

Climate is another feature usually considered by geographers when dividing countries into physical regions. The easy division in Italy is into three climatic regions (see **E**). The Mediterranean climate of 'hot, dry summers and warm, wet winters' dominates everywhere, except in the north. The most distinctive feature of a Mediterranean climate is the summer drought. In most hot parts of the world, summer is the wet season, because air rises from hot surfaces and causes thunderstorms. However, in the Mediterranean high pressure dominates in summer. The sinking air stops hot air on the ground from rising into the atmosphere.

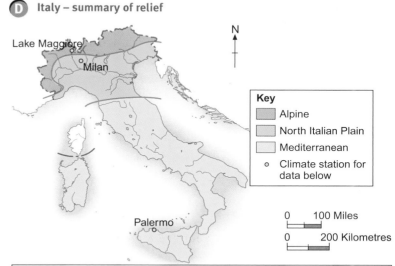

Key
- Alpine
- North Italian Plain
- Mediterranean
- o Climate station for data below

0 — 100 Miles
0 — 200 Kilometres

### Activities

**1 Odd one out.** Decide which one is the odd one out in each group and explain your choice.

   a) Alps        Apennines        Etna

   b) Adriatic    Mediterranean    Maggiore

   c) Como        Garda            Po

   d) Sardinia    Sicily           Vesuvius

**2** a) Choose *one* type of graph from *SKILLS in geography* pages 145–155 to show the data in **D**. Draw the graph.

   b) Do a class survey of types of graphs used by others.

   c) Did you make the best choice, or would another type of graph have given a better result? Explain.

**3** Use or trace an outline map of Italy.

   a) Divide Italy into *three* physical regions.

   b) Use labels or sketches to show the main features of each region.

   c) Would two or four regions have been better than three? Explain what you think.

**4** Draw a table. Use these headings to show differences between the Alps and Apennines. The photo on page 83 was taken in the Apennines.

   a) Height    b) Relief    c) Drainage (rivers and lakes)    d) Climate

**5** Think of *two* reasons why there are more rivers in the North Italian Plain than in the rest of Italy.

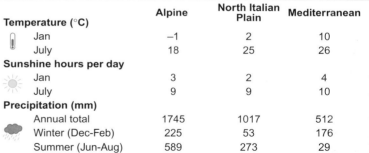

| | Alpine | North Italian Plain | Mediterranean |
|---|---|---|---|
| **Temperature (°C)** | | | |
| Jan | −1 | 2 | 10 |
| July | 18 | 25 | 26 |
| **Sunshine hours per day** | | | |
| Jan | 3 | 2 | 4 |
| July | 9 | 9 | 10 |
| **Precipitation (mm)** | | | |
| Annual total | 1745 | 1017 | 512 |
| Winter (Dec-Feb) | 225 | 53 | 176 |
| Summer (Jun-Aug) | 589 | 273 | 29 |

**E** Climatic regions of Italy

**F** Winter in the Alps

# Does Italy have a 'North and South'?

> Understanding the human geography of Italy
> Finding out how Italy can be divided into a rich North and less wealthy South

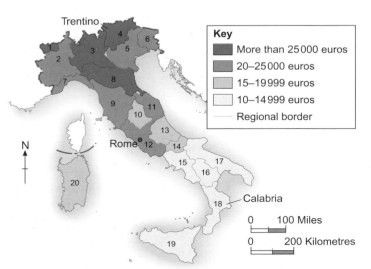

Key

| | |
|---|---|
| | More than 25 000 euros |
| | 20–25 000 euros |
| | 15–19 999 euros |
| | 10–14 999 euros |
| | Regional border |

0   100 Miles

0   200 Kilometres

**A** Income per person

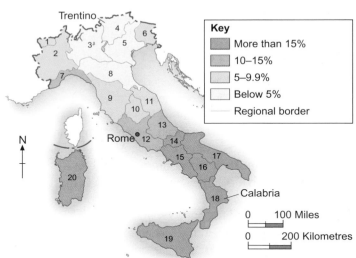

Key

| | |
|---|---|
| | More than 15% |
| | 10–15% |
| | 5–9.9% |
| | Below 5% |
| | Regional border |

0   100 Miles

0   200 Kilometres

**B** Percentage unemployed

**Names of administration regions**

| | | | |
|---|---|---|---|
| 1. Valle D'Aosta | 6. Friuli-Venezia | 11. Marche | 16. Basilicata |
| 2. Piedmont | 7. Liguria | 12. Lazio | 17. Puglia |
| 3. Lombardy | 8. Emilia-Romagna | 13. Abruzzi | 18. Calabria |
| 4. Trentino | 9. Tuscany | 14. Molise | 19. Sicily |
| 5. Veneto | 10. Umbria | 15. Campania | 20. Sardinia |

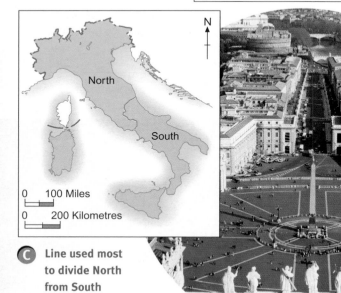

0   100 Miles

0   200 Kilometres

**C** Line used most to divide North from South

**D** View over Rome, the capital city, from St Peters in the Vatican. Most consider that the South of Italy begins south of Rome.

Some people divide the UK into a rich South and poor North. Does Italy also have a North and South?

Rich and poor are economic terms. Maps **A** and **B** were drawn to show variations between Italy's twenty administrative regions for two economic factors – income per person and percentage of people unemployed. Do the maps show that a North–South divide exists? If the divide does exist, where would you draw the line between North and South?

The gap between worst and best regions is wider in Italy than in any other EU country (**E**). The gap between North and South is so wide that the Italian government prefers to use three regions (North, Centre and South) for showing data for different areas of Italy. Check the Italian government statistics website via Hotlinks (see page 2) to find out if more up-to-date data is available.

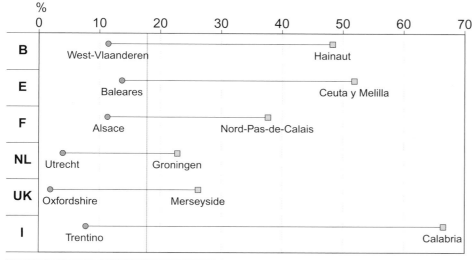

Key

| ⬤ | Lowest % | **B** | Belgium | **F** | France | **UK** | United kingdon |
| ⬜ | Highest % | **E** | Spain | **NL** | Netherlands | **I** | Italy |
| │ | Average rate for all EU countries (17.8%) | | | | | | |

**E** Best and worst youth unemployment rates inside EU countries (people under 25)

## Activities (S) 📄

1   a) Look at **A**.

    (i)   State the incomes per head in Trentino and Calabria.

    (ii)  In general, how is income per head different between North and South?

   b) Look at **B**.

    (i)   State the unemployment rates in Trentino and Calabria.

    (ii)  In general, how is the unemployment rate different between North and South?

   c) Is the North–South line in **C** drawn in the best place?

2   Look at **E**.

   a) What is the percentage difference in youth unemployment in Italy between Trentino and Calabria?

   b) State the percentage differences between highest and lowest youth unemployment rates in (i) the UK (ii) Spain.

3   a) Brainstorm with your neighbour.

    (i)   Make a list of problems caused by high rates of unemployment.

    (ii)  Think of reasons why it is really bad for young people (under 25) to be unemployed.

   b) Out of all the problems, which two do you think are more serious than the others? Explain your choices.

4   a) (i)   How is the South shown to be different from the other two regions in **F1** and **F2**?

    (ii)  Do you think that there is a link between what is shown for the South in **F1** and **F2**? Explain.

5   Study all the information on pages 84–87.

   a) Make a list of headings for differences between North and South in Italy.

   b) Draw a summary chart containing information about these differences.

1 Net migration of people in 2000

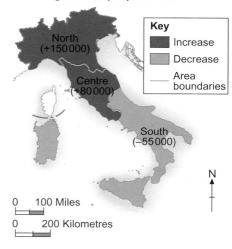

2 Percentage unemployed

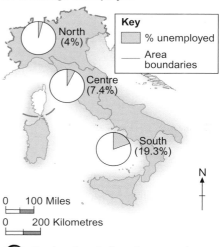

**F** Regional variations between the North, Centre and South of Italy

# Why is the North wealthy?

> Finding out about the advantages that North Italy has
> Learning about the North's main industries

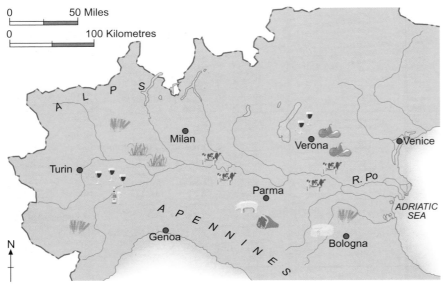

### Key

| | | | |
|---|---|---|---|
| ▼ | Wine | 🌾 | Rice |
| 🐷 | Pigs | 🌾 | Wheat |
| 🐄 | Dairy cattle | 🍎 | Orchards of fruit trees |
| 🐖 | Parma ham | 🍾 | Asti Spumante wine |
| 🧀 | Gorgonzola cheese | | |

**A** Farming on the North Italian Plain

The North Italian Plain has the best farmland and most of the modern industries. The economic core of Italy is found within what is known as its 'Industrial Triangle' between Milan, Turin and Genoa (see **C**).

## BEST FARMLAND

The northern plain has great physical advantages for farming compared with most other regions of Italy.

- Largest area of low and flat land
- Fertile soils (e.g. silt)
- Hot sunny summers with rainfall
- Plenty of water for irrigation from Alpine rivers and springs.

The large markets for food in nearby cities encouraged northern farmers to modernise and produce more. Many of Italy's most mechanised and efficient farms are located here. Cereals (wheat, rice and maize), vines and fruits (peaches, apples and pears) are the most commonly grown crops. Dairy farming is important on the wetter lands next to the River Po.

Italy is famous for food and drink – pasta, pizza, Gorgonzola and Parmesan cheeses, Parma ham, Asti wines, ice cream with many flavours. All of these are made from farm products from northern Italy. Pasta is made out of durum wheat, a variety which does not grow as well in the UK's cooler and wetter climate. How many different pasta dishes can you name?

## MOST INDUSTRY

The Northern Plain has advantages for manufacturing industry that do not exist in other parts of Italy.

- Raw materials for the many food-processing factories (**A**)
- Local or nearby supplies of power and energy (**C**)
- A pool of skilled workers created by the long history of industry and trade in many northern cities
- Wealthiest market in Italy linked by a good network of motorways (autostrade) (**C**).

**B** View of Milan from the roof of the Cathedral; the sides of the square are lined with shops filled with designer goods. Does it have the look of a wealthy city?

Its northern location, close to larger markets in other large EU countries such as Germany and France, is a big advantage today. The Alps are a formidable barrier, but there are many road and rail passes and tunnels through them (see **C**). Rail and road routes across the Alps focus on cities in the industrial triangle, and Milan in particular.

**Milan**
- Centre of clothing, food processing and light engineering industries
- Famous brands from Milan: Alfa Romeo (cars) and Necchi (sewing machines)

**Turin**
- Industry dominated by motor vehicles and engineering works making parts for cars
- Home of Fiat (cars) and Olivetti (previously typewriters, now business machines)

**Genoa**
- Main port importing fuels (crude oil, coal) and raw materials (iron ore, raw cotton)
- Mainly heavy industries (oil refineries, steel works) using imported raw materials

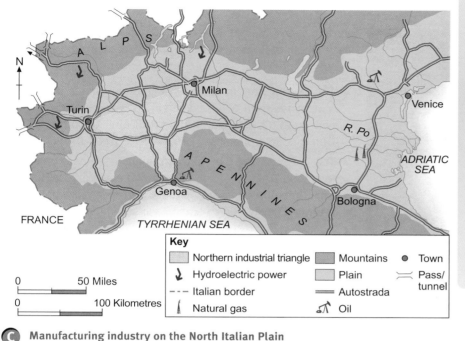

Key
- Northern industrial triangle
- Hydroelectric power
- Italian border
- Natural gas
- Mountains
- Plain
- Autostrada
- Oil
- Town
- Pass/tunnel

0    50 Miles
0    100 Kilometres

**C** Manufacturing industry on the North Italian Plain

## Activities

**1** Area of crops (thousands of hectares) in Italy:

Wheat 2200; Fodder crops for animals 1500; Olive trees 1100; Maize 1050; Tomatoes, fruit and vegetables 1000; Vines 700.

a) Draw a bar graph to show these figures.

b) Name the crop or crops used in each of the following:

   (i) pasta        (ii) wine       (iii) cooking oil

   (iv) sweetcorn   (v) pizza       (vi) spaghetti bolognaise.

**2** a) Rearrange the four physical advantages for farming on the North Italian Plain using the headings *climate, relief, drainage* and *soils*.

b) Give more details about each of them using information from **A** and earlier pages (especially pages 84–85).

**3** a) Make a larger version of **D**. Leave plenty of space for filling in the boxes.

b) Complete the diagram by filling in the five boxes with information.

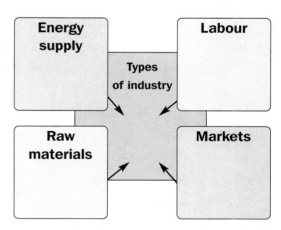

**D** Favourable factors for industry in the North

# Why is the South poor?

> Discovering the disadvantages of South Italy
> Understanding the causes behind the lack of wealth

A  A close-up view of a hilltop settlement

Visitors to the south of Italy begin to notice changes when they travel south of Rome along the main road south, the 'Autostrada del Sole' or 'motorway of the sun'.

- The midday heat in summer is greater. A fierce summer sun shines from a clear blue sky. Villages and towns go very quiet between 12.30 and 4.30pm. A good lunch with a couple of glasses of wine is followed by a 'siesta'.

- The landscape of the southern Apennines has a harsher look (see **B** on page 84). Vegetation cover is less, bare rock outcrops are more frequent and areas of cropland are mainly confined to small basins and coastal plains.

- More and more settlements are perched on hilltops, surrounded by rocky slopes (see photo on page 83). Can people make a good living here? Why don't more live on the flatter lowlands?

To explain differences between places geographers look for both physical and human factors. The causes of poverty in the south of Italy are summarised in **D**.

B  Inside a hilltop village. What are the advantages and disadvantages of living along streets like these?

C  Hilltop orchard next to the village. Is it being well farmed?

**A  Old-fashioned farming methods**

Large wheat fields with low yields

Slopes of hills grazed by sheep and goats

**B  Climate**

Fierce summer heat

Outdoor summer temperatures above 40°C

Summer drought is almost complete

**C  Drainage**

Lack of surface rivers

Dry appearance to the landscape

In summer river beds are dry

**D**  Lack of wealth in the South – physical and human causes. Can you separate the human factors from the physical?

**D  History**

Long history of being invaded

People lived in hilltop villages for defence

Marshy lowlands were avoided as places to live because malarial mosquitoes bred there

**E  Lack of modern industry**

Remote from main EU markets

Mainly unskilled labour

No cheap hydro-electric power, unlike the North

Long history of crime and corruption

**G  Relief**

Large areas of mountain and hilly land

Small percentage of plain

Steep slopes are eroded by heavy winter rain

**F  Land ownership**

Few farmers own their own land

Large landowners own big estates (*latifundi*)

Many landlords live in the cities (not on their farms)

Little money is invested in improving the land

**H  Rock type and soils**

The main rock is hard limestone

It is permeable, leaving dry surfaces

Thin soils between bare rock outcrops

## Activities

1   A family from Milan is going on their summer holiday to Naples by car. Fill in a table like the one on the right to show some of the differences they will notice between crossing the North Italian Plain and travelling in the South between Rome and Naples.

|  | Milan to Bologna | Rome to Naples |
|---|---|---|
| Weather |  |  |
| Landscape |  |  |
| Farming |  |  |

2   What is it like living in a hilltop village in southern Italy?

   a) What are the advantages during the great heat of summer?

   b) What are the problems for these people?

   (i) Old people     (ii) Young couples with families

   (iii) Delivery van drivers     (iv) Farmers

3   a) Rearrange the titles A–H in **D** under the headings 'physical' and 'human'.

   b) Rank the eight titles A–H in what you consider to be their order of importance, starting with 1 for the most important.

   c) Explain why you chose the top two.

4   a) Make a recording sheet like the one on the right.

   b) Note down the rank orders from *nine* other people in the class.

   c) Work out the average rank for each of A–H.

   d) Which are the top two now? Can you explain why they are considered to be the most important?

**Order of importance**

|  | Mine | 2 | 3 | 4 | 5 | 6 | 7 | 8 | 9 | 10 | Total | Average rank |
|---|---|---|---|---|---|---|---|---|---|---|---|---|
| A | 4 |  |  |  |  |  |  |  |  |  |  |  |
| B | 1 |  |  |  |  |  |  |  |  |  |  |  |

# Can the gap between South and North be closed?

> Finding out what Italy has done to close the gap
> Deciding how successful these measures were

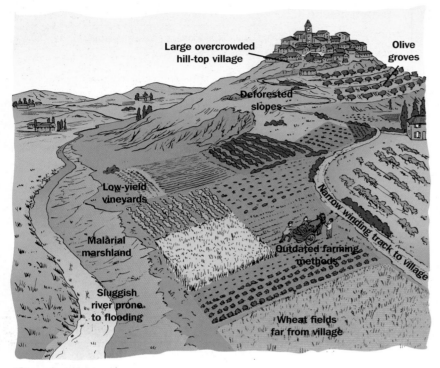

A    Landscape in the South of Italy in 1950

The government has been trying for many years to close the gap. In 1950 it set up the 'Fund for the South' (in Italian 'Cassa per il Mezzogiorno'). It began by tackling some of the problems of farming; you can see some of the many problems it faced in **A**.

## CHANGES IN FARMING IN THE SOUTH

- Large estates (*latifundi*) were broken up; land was shared out among landless peasants.
- Small dams were built across rivers, to stop flooding on the plains in winter and store irrigation water for summer use.
- Public services were improved, paved roads replaced tracks, villages and farms were linked up to mains electricity and telephones.
- Hill slopes were planted with trees; soil erosion was reduced.

Figure **B** shows how some coastal plains in the South were transformed. The low-output wheat fields and olive groves were replaced by citrus orchards (oranges, lemons, limes) and greenhouses growing salad crops (tomatoes, lettuces, cucumbers) all year round with irrigation water. These were accompanied by other important changes.

## NEW MANUFACTURING INDUSTRY

For a time in the 1960s government policy switched. It took the view that heavy industry was the key to economic growth in the South. The hope was this would have a multiplier effect – growth leading to more growth.

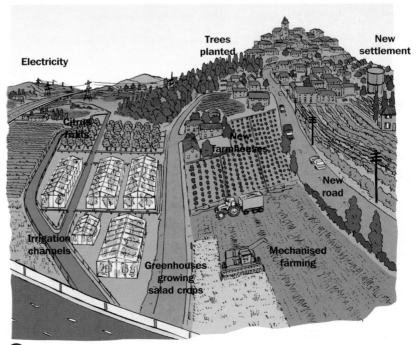

B    Landscape in the same area by 1990

Government-owned companies making steel and refining oil were forced to expand and invest in the South. The Autostrada del Sole was built, providing a fast motorway link from the South to Rome and Milan. Other industries did follow. Most were attracted by generous government grants, but they never arrived in the numbers needed to make a real difference. Some big works never attracted any other industries around them. These were called 'Cathedrals in the Desert'. Can you suggest why?

It is not surprising that some businesses failed. When car sales at Fiat slumped, it laid off workers in factories in Naples before it reduced the workforce in Turin. Do you understand why?

**A** Higher transport costs to markets in Italy and EU

C  **View from the top of the castle in a hilltop town in Sardinia. How many of the changes shown in B can you see?**

**B** Difficult to recruit skilled factory workers and office staff

**C** High rates of absenteeism, especially at harvest time for vines and olives

**D** Low output from workers not used to factory work

**E** Workers too tired to work after working on their farms before and after work

D  **Problems experienced by companies that set up in the South**

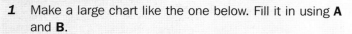

## Activities

S  A

*1*  Make a large chart like the one below. Fill it in using **A** and **B**.

|  | 1950 | 1990 |
|---|---|---|
| A  Crops grown |  |  |
| B  Farming methods used |  |  |
| C  Public services |  |  |
| (i) roads |  |  |
| (ii) other services |  |  |
| D  Settlements |  |  |
| (i) location |  |  |
| (ii) types and sizes |  |  |

**Changes in landscape and farming in the South of Italy between 1950 and 1990**

*2*  Draw a sketch of **C**. Label the new settlement, farms, orchards and other main features of the landscape.

*3*  Work in a group. The aim is to produce a list of reasons why farmers find it difficult to get used to factory work.

a) Divide out the work. Start by putting together a daily diary of work for:

(i)  two farmers, one growing crops and the other keeping animals;

(ii) two factory workers, one in a car works and another in a food-processing factory.

b) Identify the main differences between farm work and factory work.

c) Compile the list of reasons why farmers find it difficult to change to factory work. Write them out in order of importance.

d) Compare your list with those of other groups.

# Italy – a great place to visit

> **Learning about Italy as a tourist destination**

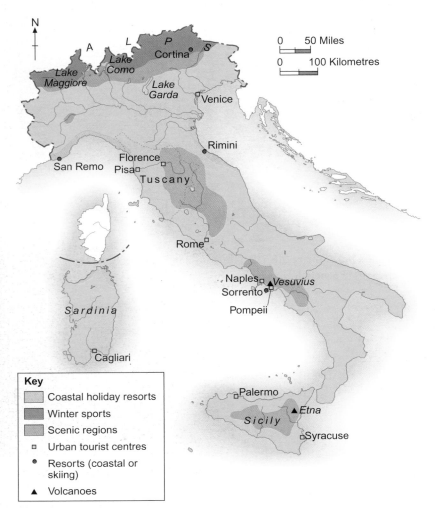

**Key**

- Coastal holiday resorts
- Winter sports
- Scenic regions
- □ Urban tourist centres
- ● Resorts (coastal or skiing)
- ▲ Volcanoes

**A** Tourism in Italy

Italy is near the top of the international tourist league table of visitors, because of its wide range of tourist attractions. Map **A** summarises what Italy has to offer.

1 Italy is a Mediterranean country. Therefore it has similar attractions for tourists as Spain and Greece. For people living in the colder and more cloudy climates further north in Europe, Italy can guarantee summer sun and warm sea – great for beach holidays.

2 Italy is also one of the Alpine countries. Although the shores of the Italian Lakes are popular with summer visitors, the peak tourist season in the Alps is winter. The steep snow-covered slopes are a winter paradise for skiers and snowboarders.

3 Italy has a rich cultural heritage. There are many reminders of its long and prosperous history, particularly in the cities of the North and Centre. Here there are spectacular Roman remains, impressive cathedrals and churches and museums full of works of art. In addition, Italy offers three unique attractions – the leaning tower of Pisa, Venice and its network of canals (see pages 96–97) and Pompeii, the Roman town preserved by its covering of ash from the volcano Vesuvius.

**B** Early morning on the beach; the sunbeds are already out, always arranged in neat rows in Italian resorts

**C** Leaning tower of Pisa: visitors like to be photographed as if they are stopping the tower from falling over

There is more. The northern Apennines may not have the scenic grandeur of the Alps, but Tuscany, with its rolling hills and farming landscapes, is very popular with British visitors. So also is Italian food and drink. Italians like their food and take great pride in the quality of their cooking (**D**). Lunch will usually be accompanied with a glass or two of wine (e.g. Chianti) and may last at least two hours.

There are some differences in the types of holidays taken by Italians in their own country and by foreign visitors (see **E**). Italians like to make for the beach in mid summer, while foreign visitors prefer the museums, art galleries and churches in the historical cities. The hot springs and volcanic areas in the south add to the variety of types of holiday that Italy has to offer (see **F** and **G**).

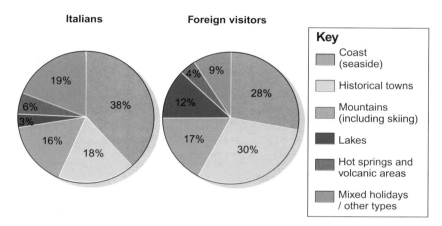

**E** Types of holidays (percentage in 2001)

## *Antipasto (Appetiser)*
Selection of cold meats and vegetables:
Prosciutto (ham), salami, olives,
artichoke hearts

## *Pasta*
Spaghetti or macaroni or ravioli

## *Main course*
Veal or chicken in a white wine or
tomato sauce

## *Dessert*
Fresh fruit or ice cream

## *Coffee*
Espresso, cappuccino, latte

**D** Lunch menu in a restaurant

**F** Mount Etna – a major tourist attraction

**G** Hot mud pools on the island of Vulcano

## Activities

1 Tourist percentages in Italy according to time of year:

January–March 17 per cent; April–June 23 per cent; July–September 43 per cent; October–December 17 per cent

a) Draw a graph or diagram to show these percentages.

b) Which *two* types of holiday area in Italy will be busiest (i) in July–September (ii) in January–March?

c) Explain your choice of answers to part (b).

2 Write out and finish these sentences.

a) ___ % more Italians than foreign visitors took seaside holidays in Italy. I think the reasons for this are …

b) ___ % more foreigners than Italians took holidays in the historical cities. I think the reasons for this are …

c) The place in Italy I would most like to visit is _____ , because …

d) The type of holiday in Italy that I would enjoy least is _____ , because …

3 Working in pairs, design a poster with the title: 'Italy – a great place to visit'. Use holiday brochures and websites to help you.

# Venice and that sinking feeling

> Understanding the physical geography behind Venice's sinking feeling

> Looking at what human geography can do to help Venice

Venice is built on over 100 islands at the northern end of the Adriatic Sea (**A**). The Grand Canal 'meanders' its way through the centre of the city, with canals leading from it in all directions (**B**). A large sand bar (the Lido) separates the sheltered waters of the lagoon from the Adriatic Sea. The road and railway, which are connected to Venice from the mainland by a causeway, stop at the city's edge. The easiest way to travel around Venice is by boat, either using the famous gondolas or the *vaporetti* (water buses). Jobs done by van and lorry in other cities, such as delivering goods and collecting waste, are done by boat in Venice.

MESTRE

VENICE

Port
Marghera

The Lido

A D R I A T I C

S E A

N

0    5 Kilometres

**Key**
- Built up areas
- ++++ Railway
- Causeway
- Deep water channel
- Sand bar
- Reclaimed land
- Mud flats

**(A)** Location of Venice

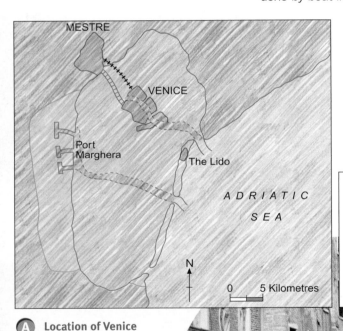

**(C)** One of the 'back streets' in Venice; some of the buildings standing in the water are beginning to show their age

**(B)** The Grand Canal, the 'main street' of Venice, busy with water traffic

Why build a city in the middle of mudflats? It seems like a crazy idea, but for merchants in fourteenth century Venice it made good sense. The site was easy to defend while still allowing direct access to the sea for trade. Venetian merchants made fortunes and spent the money on fine mansions (called palaces), churches and bridges. Artists were hired to decorate the insides of buildings with paintings and mosaics. What remains is a city full of artistic and architectural treasures.

# VENICE'S PROBLEMS

The sea, which originally brought wealth to Venice, is now the main cause of its problems. However, the sea cannot be blamed for everything (see **D**). The organisation Venice in Peril warns that without any action the city will be uninhabitable by 2100. You can visit the Venice in Peril website via Hotlinks (see page 2).

# SOLUTIONS TO THE PROBLEMS?

Many people ask: 'Why was something like the Thames Barrage not built many years ago?' Italian governments are not known for making quick decisions. Countless suggestions have been made without any action. The current favourite is a system of 'floating gates' (see **E**). Three large gates will be built that lie folded flat on the sea bed next to each of the three inlets into the lagoon (see **A**). When the water level rises by one metre or more, air will be pumped into each gate, causing one end to float upwards and block any surges of water during storms. The estimated cost is at least £1.6 billion.

However, this solution raises other issues. What will be the economic and environmental effects of closing the three entrances to the lagoon on 100 days a year? How will Port Marghera be affected? Where will the sewage go?

---

**Venice is sinking!**
23 cm since 1900:
- 13 cm caused by subsidence
- 10 cm caused by rising sea levels
Current rate 1–1.5 mm per year

**Subsidence**
Venice is settling into the mudflats
- Cause – weight of buildings on soft foundations

**Sea levels are rising!**
Rising since the end of the Great Ice Age (about 10 000 years ago)
- Speeding up because of global warming
- Some people are estimating a sea level rise of 60 cm between 2000 and 2100

**Flooding**
Regular winter floods in central area, e.g. St Mark's Square
- 1900 – 10 floods a year     • 2000 – 100 floods a year

**Buildings are crumbling**
Stonework rots in the smoggy, acid air and polluted water
- Main cause – chemical works in Port Marghera (see A)
- Other cause – inefficient sewage system

**People are leaving**
Population 60 per cent lower than 50 years ago
- Ground floors of buildings abandoned as living quarters due to dampness
- One in twelve buildings is empty
- Buildings are rotting away because of rising damp and no repair work

**D** The problems of Venice and their causes

---

## Activities  (S) (📄) (A)

**1** **Group activity** – prepare a presentation on 'Why Venice must be saved', supported by leaflets and handouts. Pool ideas, share out the work and look at websites for up-to-date information (e.g. Hotlinks see page 2). Possible headings for the work include:

- How Venice is unique/different
- Present problems of Venice
- Why the problems are getting worse/why action is needed more urgently than ever

**2** a) Describe how the floating gates would work.

   b) Draw a sketch map to show where the gates would be placed.

   c) Show the possible advantages and disadvantages of the gates on spider diagrams. Look at *SKILLS in geography* pages 145–155 for help with this.

   d) Should the gates be built? Explain your view.

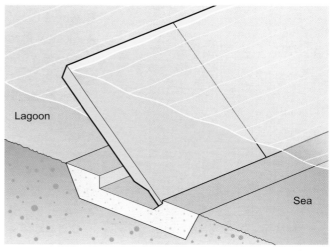

**E** How floating gates might save Venice from flooding

# An ageing population – Italy's economic time bomb

> Finding out why an ageing population is a problem
> Looking at possible economic solutions

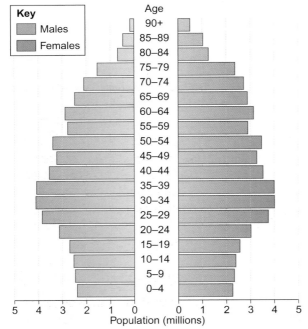

**A** Population pyramid for Italy (in 2001)

Key
- Males
- Females

Age
90+
85–89
80–84
75–79
70–74
65–69
60–64
55–59
50–54
45–49
40–44
35–39
30–34
25–29
20–24
15–19
10–14
5–9
0–4

5 4 3 2 1 0 0 1 2 3 4 5
Population (millions)

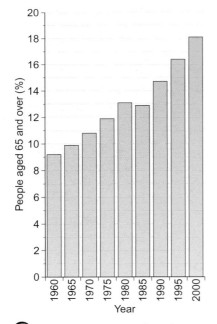

**B** Italy – percentage of total population aged 65 and above

**Fertility rates** are low throughout Europe and falling. The fertility rate is the number of children per woman. In 1970 women in Western Europe were having on average 2.4 children. By 2003 this had dropped to 1.5. The reasons are the same in all EU countries.

- Women are better educated and want to pursue their own careers.
- Women are marrying and having their first babies when they are older.

A fertility rate of 2.1 children per woman is needed for a country to maintain the same total population. Italy's fertility rate in 2003 was 1.3, joint lowest in the EU with Spain. Look at the population pyramid for Italy (see **A**). How does it show that fertility rates have been falling for 30 years? What was the percentage of people aged 65 and older in 2001?

Does it matter that fertility rates are falling in Italy? There are expected to be six million fewer Italians by 2050. If Italy's wealth is shared among fewer people, all Italians should be better off.

## AGEING POPULATION AND PENSIONS

Italy has an **ageing population**; the percentage of old people (aged 65 and over) is increasing (see **B**). The problem facing all Italian governments is how to find the money to pay state pensions to more and more people.

### Questions and answers about pensions

**Q** Where do governments get the money to pay out pensions?

**A** Most of it comes out of taxes.

**Q** Who pays most money in tax?

**A** Working people (mainly those aged 16–64). They pay income tax and a percentage of what they earn in insurance contributions.

**Q** Don't governments have a 'pot of money' for paying out pensions?

**A** No. State pensions are paid out on a 'pay-as-you-go' basis. This means that money now being collected in taxes and insurance contributions from working people is paid straight out to pensioners.

**Q** Isn't this system unfair to all the workers?

**A** When the people who are now pensioners were working, they did the same. Some of the tax they paid was given in pensions to people who were over 65 and retired. This is just the way it works.

So, if it has always worked like this, why is a big pensions problem now looming in Italy? Pensions are taking an ever-increasing percentage of Italy's GDP (total income each year).

| Year | Number of working age (15–64) for every person 65 years old and older | Estimates for pension costs as a percentage of GDP |
|------|------|------|
| 2000 | 4.3 | 12.6 |
| 2010 | 3.8 | 13.2 |
| 2020 | 3.3 | 15.3 |
| 2030 | 2.8 | 20.3 |
| 2040 | 2.4 | 21.4 |

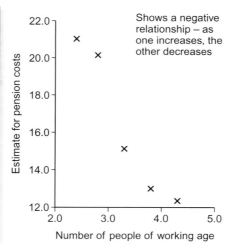

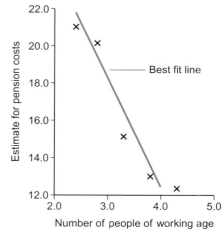

 **C** Future pensions crisis in Italy

When the values for the number of working people per pensioner are plotted against future estimates of pension costs in **C**, a negative relationship is shown. In other words, pension costs will increase as the number of workers per pensioner decreases.

## Activities

**1** Use **A**.

   a) What percentage are under 15?

   b) What percentage are 65 and over?

   c) Are there similar percentages of males and females within these two groups?

**2** a) What is a pension?

   b) How are pensions paid for?

   c) Why do people in Italy and other EU countries expect a pension when they retire?

   d) Write a paragraph to explain why a pension crisis is likely in Italy before 2050.

**3** a) Draw a scatter graph to show the values for Italy in **D**.

   b) Describe what your graph shows.

| Year | Fertility rate | Percentage aged 65 and over |
|------|------|------|
| 1960 | 2.4 | 9.2 |
| 1970 | 2.3 | 10.8 |
| 1980 | 1.6 | 13.1 |
| 1990 | 1.3 | 14.7 |
| 2000 | 1.3 | 18.1 |

 **D**

### Key words

**Ageing population** – increasing percentage of old people (aged 65 and over) in a country

**Fertility rate** – average number of children born to a woman in her lifetime

### SKILLS

**How to draw a scatter graph**

1 Draw the two axes for the graph.

2 Label the two axes.

3 Choose suitable scales to cover the range of values.

4 Place a cross or dot at the point where the two values meet.

5 Do not join up the dots.

6 If possible, draw a straight line which is the 'best fit' for all the points.

*For more help* see page 149 of *SKILLS in geography*.

# Pensions time bomb in the EU – what can governments do?

**A** Road traffic sign – a warning for motorists. What about for governments?

**Possible options for governments**

**A** **Raise the age of retirement – from 65 to 70, or even to 75**
- Increase the length of time people are working and paying taxes.
- Reduce the number of years of life for people to draw a state pension.

**B** **Encourage couples to have more children – raise the fertility rate to above 2.1**
- Increase length of maternity leave from work with full pay.
- Increase length of paternity leave and make it paid leave as well.
- Improve childcare and nursery facilities for the under-fives, making them cheaper and more widely available.

**C** **Allow more immigrants to come in – especially those aged between 20 and 40**
- Issue more visas and work permits to people living in countries outside the EU.
- Fill in gaps in the job market and collect taxes on money earned.

**D** **Reduce state pensions – workers take out private pension plans with insurance companies**
- Transfer responsibility for pensions from the state to the workers.
- Money problem for government reduced if pensions go down at the same time as income from taxes.

1 Look at **A**.
  a) Why are both groups shown on the road sign expensive for governments?
  b) Why do governments like people in the age group in between?
2 Something will have to be done about the pensions time bomb. Doing nothing is not an option. Which of the options do you prefer?
  a) Draw a line like the one below with a scale of 1 to 10. Place letters for options A–D to show what you think about each option.

  **Very bad idea** 1 _____ 10 **Very good idea**

  b) Explain your choice of best and worst options.
3 Draw two more lines. Choose *two* people from the list below.
  - Worker aged 55
  - Owner of a small company with ten workers
  - Manager of a big insurance company
  - Newly married couple in their 20s
  a) Show what they are likely to think of the four options.
  b) Suggest reasons for probable differences in views between them.

# >> 7    Rich world, poor world

Can you imagine how much a flat costs here? It is the world's greatest concentration of buildings in the world's richest country. Why should there be so much wealth here while other parts of the world are so poor?

## *Learning objectives*

What are you going to learn about in this chapter?

> The differences between a rich country and a poor country
> Where rich and poor countries are located
> Different ways to measure wealth and development
> Physical and human reasons why some countries remain poor
> Why sub-Saharan Africa is the world's poorest region
> How small changes can greatly improve the quality of life for poor people
> Whether poor countries are caught in a trade and poverty trap

**A** Manhattan, New York

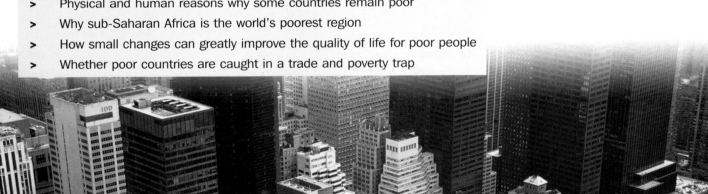

# Are you rich or poor?

> Looking at the differences between rich and poor
> Finding out how to use the US dollar to compare wealth

| Item | Value |
|---|---|
| Pay-as-you-go mobile | £65 |
| MiniDisc player | £120 |
| GameBoy Advance | £90 |
| Games, each game | £30 |
| Nike trainers | £75 |
| Bag | £20 |
| Total | £400 |

**A** What a typical teenager in the UK carries (approximate UK prices in 2004)

Are you rich or poor? Some of you will answer 'poor', probably because you do not have enough money for all that you would like to buy. Take a look at **A**. How many of the items in the list do you own? Some people say that today's UK teenagers and students are the wealthiest ever. What is the total for you when you include the clothes that you wear outside school as well?

Now look at **B**. The UN (United Nations) estimates that one in every five people in the world lives in extreme poverty on less than one US dollar (60–90 pence) per day (see **C**). Does it come as a surprise to you that anyone can live on one dollar a day? This includes everything needed for survival – food, shelter and clothing. No one can live on this amount in the UK, so the way of life of these people must be very different.

Many of those living on less than a dollar a day are farmers who grow most, if not all, of their own food. They also build their own homes and many make their own clothes, sometimes from the wool of their own animals. All the family are expected to help collect wood for cooking and heating, usually the only source of energy available.

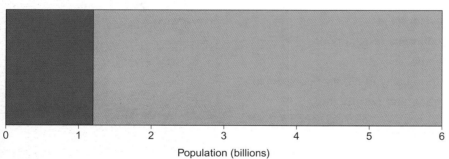

Population (billions)

Map **D** shows where the greatest concentrations of poor people are found. You can see clearly that sub-Saharan Africa is the world's poorest region; it includes all the continent of Africa except for the five countries that border the Mediterranean Sea. Half the population are living on less than a dollar a day.

**B** People living on less than US $1 per day in 2000

**Key**
■ People living on less than US $1 a day
■ People living on more than US $1 a day

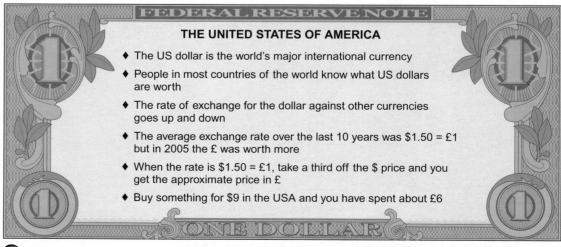

## THE UNITED STATES OF AMERICA

♦ The US dollar is the world's major international currency
♦ People in most countries of the world know what US dollars are worth
♦ The rate of exchange for the dollar against other currencies goes up and down
♦ The average exchange rate over the last 10 years was $1.50 = £1 but in 2005 the £ was worth more
♦ When the rate is $1.50 = £1, take a third off the $ price and you get the approximate price in £
♦ Buy something for $9 in the USA and you have spent about £6

**C** US dollars

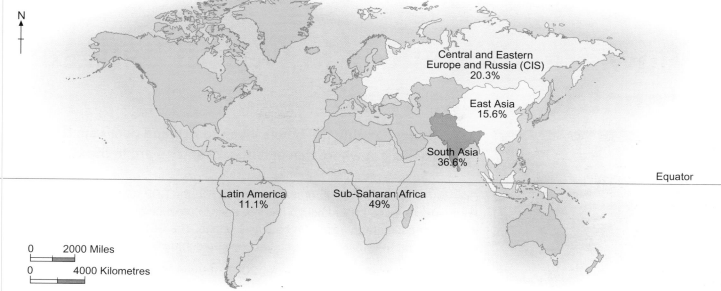

N

**D** **People living on less than US $1 per day in 2000 (%)**

In some places rich and poor live close together. Look at photo **E**. A self-built home on the beach in Mumbai (Bombay) in India is next to the apartment blocks and hotels for rich people and businessmen.

## Activities **S**

Look at *SKILLS in geography* pages 145–155 for help with these activities.

**1** a) Draw a pictograph to show that one out of every five people in the world lives on less than a dollar a day.

b) Use a bar graph to display the percentages given in **D**.

**2** a) Trace or sketch an outline map of the continent of Africa. Shade in and name sub-Saharan Africa.

b) How does **D** show that sub-Saharan Africa is the world's poorest region by a large margin?

**3** a) Make a list of all the signs of poverty and wealth shown in photo **E**.

b) Make a large frame and draw a sketch of **E**. Use the list you made to label your sketch.

**4** Some African farmers were asked: 'What gives you a feeling of wealth and well-being?' Their answers included:

• Fertile land for growing crops

• Healthy cattle and goats

• Good roofs on homes to keep the rain out

• Children or relatives working abroad and sending back money

• Owning a fridge, TV and bicycle

• Good neighbours who will give help when needed.

a) Work in pairs. Think about the answers that someone living in the UK might have given to the same question. Write down *six* likely answers.

b) Explain why you would expect the UK answers to be different.

**E** **Beach living in Mumbai**

# How are differences in wealth between countries measured?

> Understanding the labels given to rich and poor countries
> Looking at where rich and poor countries are in the world

**A** The value of goods sold at markets like this one in Ecuador in South America is unlikely to be included in the country's GDP

One way to show the wealth of a country is to use the GDP (Gross Domestic Product) (see page 12). Although it is not easy to produce accurate data, the GDP is the best estimate there is of a country's wealth. The GDP is always stated in US dollars so that the wealth of one country can be compared with that of another.

When GDP calculations were done for 2003, the top three countries were:

| | | |
|---|---|---|
| 1 | Luxembourg | US $41 950 per head |
| 2 | Norway | US $37 020 per head |
| 3 | USA | US $35 200 per head |

Luxembourg and Norway have small populations, whereas the USA's wealth had to be shared between its 290 million people. The USA is the world's richest large country. The UK was twelfth with a GDP per head of US $23 920.

Three of the four lowest GDPs per head in 2003 were for countries in sub-Saharan Africa – Congo with US $100, Ethiopia with US $100 and Burundi with US $110. It is difficult to produce accurate GDPs for these countries because many people are poor farmers who just grow enough to eat. They are called **subsistence** farmers. No money value is given to what they produce.

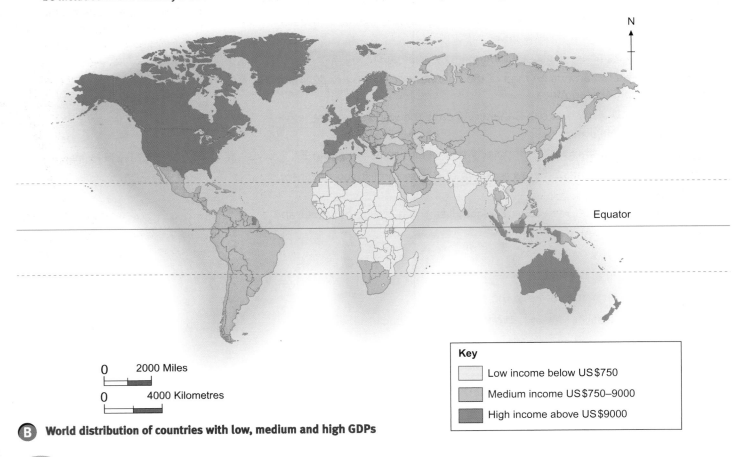

N

Equator

**Key**

Low income below US $750

Medium income US $750–9000

High income above US $9000

**B** World distribution of countries with low, medium and high GDPs

0     2000 Miles

0     4000 Kilometres

# DIVIDING THE WORLD INTO RICH AND POOR

In Book 1 you looked at physical divisions of the world into northern and southern hemispheres and continents and oceans. But in human geography the most commonly used division is between rich and poor. The dividing line is shown in map **C**. Notice how the line runs west to east through the northern hemisphere for most of its course, until it make a dramatic change in direction off the coast of Asia. It makes a loop around Australia so that Japan, Australia and New Zealand are included with the other rich countries on the 'northern' side of the line.

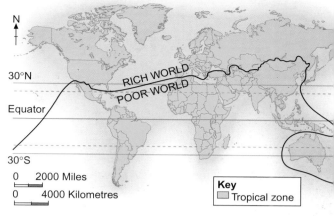

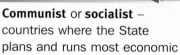 The dividing line between rich and poor countries

Compare the course taken by the line in map **C** with what map **B** shows about differences in the wealth of countries based on GDP. How neatly does the line split the world into rich and poor? Where is the divide between rich and poor very clear? Where is it less clear?

Several different labels are used for this human division of the world into rich and poor:

- 'North' and 'South'
- 'First World' and 'Third World'
- '**MEDCs**' (More Economically Developed Countries) and '**LEDCs**' (Less Economically Developed Countries).

Rich countries are concentrated in the temperate zone in North America and Europe, well *north* of the Equator. Poor countries lie further *south*, many of them in the tropical zone and in the southern hemisphere in continents such as Africa and South America.

When looking at the labels 'First World' and 'Third World', the obvious question is 'What has happened to the 'Second World'?'. The answer is that it has largely disappeared. The 'Second World' was made up of **socialist** countries. Until the collapse of **communist** governments in the Soviet Union and Eastern Europe in the 1990s, most people in these countries had incomes between those in the rich North and poor South. These countries are now included in the 'First World'.

The third set of labels is the one used most in geography today – MEDCs for rich developed countries and LEDCs for poor developing countries. You'll find out more about them on the next page.

You'll find out more about them on the next page.

## Key words

**Communist** or **socialist** – countries where the State plans and runs most economic activities

**LEDCs** – Less Economically Developed Countries; the poorer countries of the world

**MEDCs** – More Economically Developed Countries; the richer countries of the world

**Subsistence** – living on what a family grows and produces for itself

## Activities

1. What does map **B** shows about wealth in:
   a) Europe?  b) Africa?

2. a) Describe the course followed by the line in map **C** dividing rich and poor worlds.

   b) Look at maps **B** and **C**.

   (i) Name *two* places where differences in wealth between rich and poor are very clear on the two sides of the line.

   (ii) Name *one* place where the difference is less clear.

   c) How useful is the line for making a simple division of the world into rich and poor? Explain your answer.

# What is development?

> Looking at how development can be measured
> Discovering the difference between 'standard of living' and 'quality of life'

## Key words

**Development** – level of growth and wealth of a country

**Human development index (HDI)** – a measure of the level of development calculated on the average income, life expectancy and literacy rate of a country's population

**Literacy rate** – percentage of adults who can read and write

**Quality of life** – how well someone can live, including health and education as well as wealth

**Standard of living** – how well off and wealthy a person is

**Development** means change and growth in a country, and normally an increase in wealth. This is why more economically developed countries (MEDCs), such as the USA, UK, Japan and Australia, are part of the rich world 'north' of the line in **C** on page 105. These are the industrialised countries that generate enough wealth to give most of their citizens a high **standard of living**. After spending money on essentials such as food, clothing and shelter, the majority of people in these countries have money left for buying luxury goods or taking holidays. However, there is more to development than becoming richer; it is also about improving people's **quality of life**.

All countries want economic development, but some have moved further along the road of development than others. Graph **A** shows the GDPs for a sample of countries from very poor to very rich. In fact, they are all countries beginning with the letter 'S' and having more than one million people. Sierra Leone (US $160) had the fifth lowest GDP in the world in 2003, while Switzerland (US $34 460) had the fifth highest. Countries with GDPs below about US $9000 are usually included among the less economically developed countries (LEDCs).

Some LEDCs are developing quickly; these are known as Newly Industrialising Countries (NICs). South Korea (in Asia) is a good example; its manufacturing industry has grown very quickly in the past 40 years. Singapore used to be an NIC but is now an MEDC.

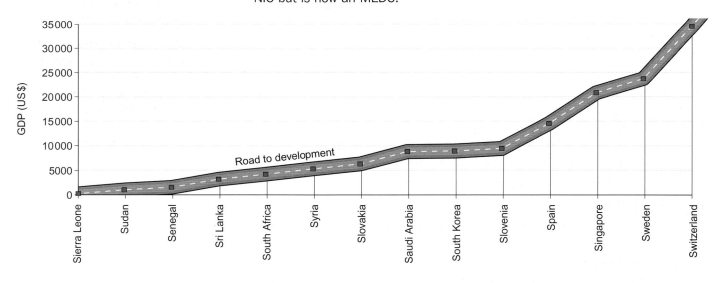

**A** The road to development – GDPs for a sample of countries from poor to rich

## HUMAN DEVELOPMENT INDEX

Money may not be everything, but everyone knows that it helps! The **human development index** (HDI) uses average income per head, but also takes into account two other factors that strongly affect a person's quality of life, life expectancy and **literacy rate**. Data from the three measures are combined in an index that gives a wider view of development. Map **B** shows the world distribution of countries with low, medium and high levels of human development.

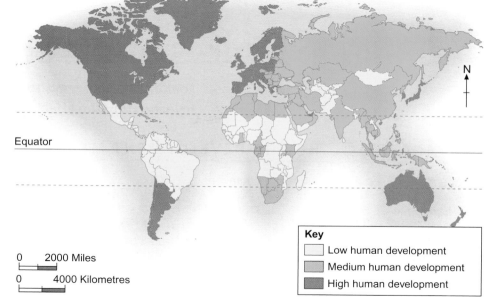

Equator

0     2000 Miles

0     4000 Kilometres

**Key**

☐ Low human development

▨ Medium human development

▪ High human development

**B**   World distribution of countries with low, medium and high human development

Look back at map **B** on page 104. How similar is the picture of world wealth and development on the two maps? How many countries can you find with high human development on the southern side of the dividing line between rich and poor? There are some. One is the UAE (United Arab Emirates), an oil-rich state in the Gulf. Another is Argentina in South America, a country with levels of literacy and life expectancy similar to those in MEDCs.

What is meant by 'poor' is not necessarily the same in both LEDCs and MEDCs. In LEDCs, the most pressing poverty issues are:

- **hunger**   • **illiteracy**   • **disease**   • **lack of health services**
- **no access to safe water**

In MEDCs, hunger is rare, literacy rates are close to 100 per cent, epidemics of disease are well controlled, health services are available to all and safe water comes from the taps in homes, therefore other issues are more important. In the UK, groups considered to be poorer than the rest are pensioners, single parents, the unemployed and the homeless. What poverty issues matter most to people in these groups?

## Top of human development league

**Norway** (northern Europe)
Annual income per person
US $30 000
Life expectancy 79 years
Literacy rate 100 per cent

## Bottom of human development league

**Sierra Leone** (West Africa)
Annual income per person
US $470
Life expectancy 34 years
Literacy rate 33 per cent

**C**   Two extremes of HDI

## Activities

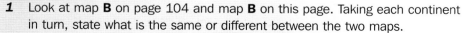

**1**   Look at map **B** on page 104 and map **B** on this page. Taking each continent in turn, state what is the same or different between the two maps.

**2**   Think about the likely differences in quality of life between people living in Norway and Sierra Leone, e.g. life expectancy, GDP.

**3**   Work in groups.

    a) Write down your ideas about what makes for (i) high and (ii) low standard of living in the UK.

    b) Choose what you consider to be the best five ideas for each of high and low standard of living. Show them on two spider diagrams (see *SKILLS in geography*, pages 145–155 for help with this).

    c) Can you make links between your ideas and different groups of people who might be particularly affected, e.g. pensioners?

# Other measures of development

> Looking at other ways to measure development in a country
> Investigating the effects of poverty

## FACT FILE  HOW IS DEVELOPMENT MEASURED?

Figure **A** shows some different ways to compare development.

**Economic**
GDP per head
LEDC US $2904          MEDC US $15 986
Percentage working in farming
LEDC 61 per cent          MEDC 10 per cent

**Education**
Adult literacy rate
LEDC 70 per cent          MEDC 99 per cent
Percentage of children not attending primary school
LEDC 22 per cent          MEDC 0 per cent

**Health**
Life expectancy at birth
LEDC 61.8 years          MEDC 74.1 years
Percentage of people with access to safe water
LEDC 71 per cent          MEDC 99 per cent

**A** Measures of development

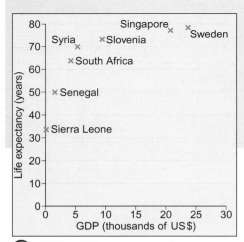

**B** GDP and life expectancy for countries with different levels of development

It is often possible to find a relationship between a country's wealth, as shown by the GDP, and the other measures of development (see **A**). The scatter graph is one of the most useful ways of showing relationships (see **B**). Notice how, as GDP increases, so also does life expectancy. This shows a positive relationship between them.

## WHAT DOES THE GREAT DEVELOPMENT DIVIDE MEAN?

Many of the measures of development have other effects. Take, for example, the case of poor people without clean water to drink. They will suffer more frequently from water-related diseases such as typhoid and diarrhoea. Then people become too weak to work because they are unwell with fever. This is an economic effect.

Not being able to spend as much time growing crops on their plots reduces food production. Already poor, they become poorer still and trapped in the poverty cycle shown in **C**. Once trapped, it is not easy to escape.

From time to time charity workers undertake surveys among people living in the countryside in LEDCs. One of the questions they asked villagers in sub-Saharan Africa and Asia was:

'What does poverty mean for you?'

The most common answers were:

'Not enough farm land'

'Having bad housing'

'Having to send our children out to work'

'Short of livestock and farm equipment'

'Not being able to send children to school'

'Not owning the land we farm'

'Being single parents'

'Having more mouths to feed'

'Not having enough healthy people in the family to care for the rest of us'

'Having food security for only a few months each year after the harvest'

If farmers and other people living in villages in the UK were asked the same question, what answers would you expect? Are any of them likely to be the same?

**Poverty cycle diagram:**

Poverty → Have only unsafe water to drink → Diseases common → Less able to work → Less food provided → Poverty

**C** Poverty cycle

## Activities

**1**  a) The difference in GDP between MEDCs and LEDCs is US $13 082. Work out the differences for the other five measures of development in **A**.

   b) Rank the differences from most important (1) to least important (6). Compare your ranking with your neighbour and discuss the differences.

   c) Give reasons for choosing your final top two.

**2**  Draw a flow diagram starting with 'Poverty' in a box at the top and four more boxes, similar to the one in **C**. Choose the best order for the four statements and fill the boxes.

**Little contribution to family income**  **Unable to read and write**

**Cannot afford to send children to school**  **Do not have the skills needed to get a well paid job**

**3**  a) Draw a scatter graph to show GDP and percentage of people who are literate.

   b) Explain what your graph shows. Look at *SKILLS in geography*, pages 145–155 for help with this.

| Country | GDP (US $) | % literate | Country | GDP (US $) | % literate |
|---|---|---|---|---|---|
| Niger | 170 | 16 | Mali | 230 | 26 |
| Bangladesh | 1 330 | 40 | Egypt | 3 850 | 55 |
| Libya | 6 125 | 75 | Argentina | 8 900 | 96 |
| Spain | 14 500 | 98 | Canada | 22 400 | 99 |

**4**  a) Draw the same type of a sketch as the one in **A** for a farming or village scene in the UK.

   b) Label the main ways in which the UK scene is different.

   c) Write a paragraph to explain why most of the answers given by African and Asian farmers in the text do not apply in the UK.

# Why are poor countries poor?

> Finding out about the physical problems of living in the tropics
> Learning about natural hazards and their long-term effects

**A** Soil erosion after rainforest clearance in Malaysia

One reason that poor countries are poor is geographical location. Most LEDCs are tropical countries; look at **C** on page 105 – can you find any LEDCs with large areas of land in temperate latitudes? In the tropics it is hot enough to grow crops all year, not just in summer as in temperate latitudes – so why should living in the tropics be linked with poverty?

## PHYSICAL PROBLEMS FOR PEOPLE LIVING IN THE TROPICS

The temperature may not change much in the tropics, but the amount of rainfall does. Around the Equator, where it is hot and wet, the land is covered by dense rainforests. After forest clearance, tropical soils are quickly eroded and washed away by heavy tropical downpours (photo **A**). Cut off from their supplies of new nutrients from dead leaves and branches, tropical soils soon become infertile.

Around the two tropics are hot deserts, some of the driest places on Earth. What chance do people have of living here? The answer is 'none', unless fresh water can be found underground or taken from a surface river.

Variations in rainfall amounts lead to the occurrence of **natural hazards** such as **drought**, flood and violent storms, which are more widespread and devastating than in temperate lands.

---

### FACT FILE — TROPICAL STORMS AS AN EXAMPLE OF A NATURAL HAZARD

Map **B** shows places most at risk from **tropical storms**. *Hurricanes, cyclones* and *typhoons* are names used for tropical storms in different parts of the world. The only MEDCs regularly at risk from the worst effects of these are Japan and small areas in the USA and Australia.

No weather event is more frightening than a tropical storm. Wind speeds are often above 150 mph (240 km per hour). With violent winds like these, crops, trees, buildings and power lines will be destroyed, no matter what preparations people make. The wild forces of nature are just too strong.

Similarly, with downpours of 250 mm of rain or more in less than 24 hours, flooding is inevitable. The best flood-control systems in the world cannot stop it happening.

In September 2004 Hurricane Ivan spread terror and destruction through the Caribbean. You can find out about the devastation it caused in **C** and **D**; it is not surprising that it was given the name 'Ivan the Terrible'.

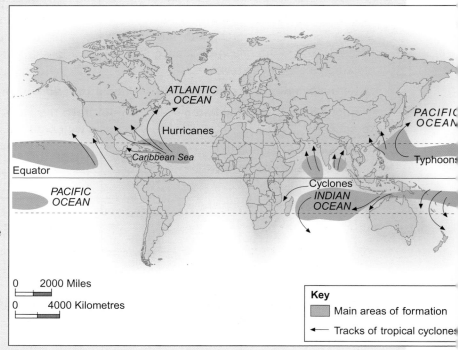

**B** Tropical storms – main zones of activity

Key
- Main areas of formation
- ← Tracks of tropical cyclones

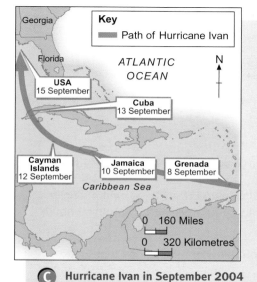

Key
■ Path of Hurricane Ivan

Georgia
Florida
ATLANTIC
OCEAN
N ↑
USA
15 September
Cuba
13 September
Cayman
Islands
12 September
Jamaica
10 September
Grenada
8 September
Caribbean Sea

0    160 Miles
0    320 Kilometres

**C** Hurricane Ivan in September 2004

**D** Grenada, 10 September 2004 – what 90 per cent hurricane devastation looks like

**10 SEPT**

# HURRICANE IVAN WRECKS GRENADA

90 per cent of houses destroyed, 60 000 homeless. The Spice Island looks like a wasteland of ruined properties and damaged vegetation.

British holidaymaker: 'I was expecting a quiet Caribbean holiday, with the sun, sand and sea promised in the brochure. What I got was a night of noise and sheer terror.'

Grenadian who had lost everything: 'I used to live in paradise. Now I have nothing – no home, no possessions, no food, no money. Who can help me?'

**11 SEPT    JAMAICA IN FEAR OF IVAN'S ARRIVAL – WINDS UP TO 150 MPH (240 KM PER HOUR) EXPECTED**

**12 SEPT    IVAN THE TERRIBLE TAKES ANGER OUT ON JAMAICA**

**13 SEPT    155 MPH (250 KM PER HOUR) WINDS AND WAVES 2 METRES HIGH BATTER THE CAYMAN ISLANDS**

CUBA gets ready for Ivan's arrival: government orders evacuation of half a million people from the western tip of the island. Cubans

instructed to store essential supplies of food and water, board up windows and move to hurricane shelters.

**E** Newspaper headlines and reports about Hurricane Ivan

## Activities

**1** Percentage loss of life from different natural hazards, 1975–2000:

Drought 50 per cent    Tropical storms 20 per cent    Earthquakes 15 per cent
Floods 10 per cent    Others 5 per cent

a) Draw a pie graph to show these percentages. Look at *SKILLS in geography*, pages 145–155 for help with this. Finish it off with a title and key.

b) Explain how these percentages show that people living in the tropics are at greatest risk from natural hazards.

**2** a) Describe the physical problems that make it difficult for people to live in a desert.

b) Draw a sketch from photo **A**. Label the problems for people that it shows.

**3** a) Draw or use a large sketch map to show the route taken by Hurricane Ivan through the Caribbean.

b) Add to your map some details of the death and destruction that resulted.

**4** a) What were the similarities and differences between the storms which affected the UK in October 2000 (see pages 40–41 of Chapter 3) and Hurricane Ivan in the Caribbean?

b) Write a paragraph to explain why storms have more serious effects on poor tropical countries like Grenada than on rich temperate countries like the UK.

**5** Is any part of the world being affected by tropical storms at present? Follow the links on Hotlinks (see page 2) and write down the details that you find.

### Key words

**Drought** – period of dry weather beyond that normally expected

**Natural hazard** – short-term event that is a danger to life and property

**Tropical storm** – area of very low pressure with high winds and heavy rainfall

# Other problems for people living in the tropics

> Learning about diseases in the tropics
> Understanding how poor health and poverty are linked

Insects and bacteria love hot, wet, tropical climates. They thrive and multiply quickly. The long list of diseases widespread in the tropics that damage human health includes:

- malaria, yellow fever, dengue fever – from bites of mosquitoes that breed in water
- cholera, typhoid, hepatitis – from drinking contaminated water
- bilharzias, guinea worm infection – from carriers that live in water.

Notice that all these diseases are in some way connected with water. The risk of people catching them increases in the wet season. This is unfortunate since it is the busiest time of the year for farmers. It is seed-sowing time, and if the farmer is not fully fit, the family's food supply for the year will be reduced.

## FACT FILE    MALARIA

This is a dangerous disease that affects more than 45 per cent of the world's population in almost 100 countries; it is a major health problem in countries in sub-Saharan Africa (pages 114–115).

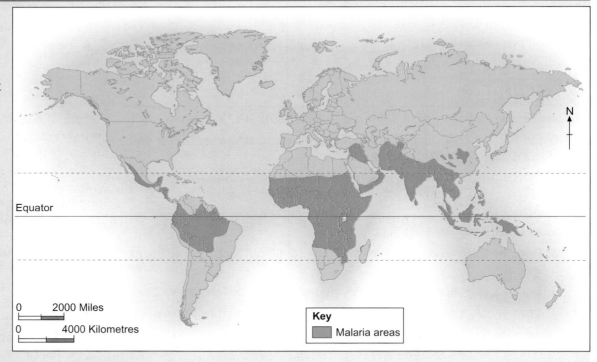

Equator

0        2000 Miles

0        4000 Kilometres

**Key**
Malaria areas

**A** Malaria – main areas affected

Mosquitoes breed in stagnant water. The most likely time for the mosquito to bite and suck a person's blood is at night. If that person's blood already contains the malaria parasite, malaria is transferred to the next person that the mosquito bites. The more people in an area that have malaria, the faster its spread will be.

- Malaria kills 2.7 million people a year.
- 75 per cent of these are African children under the age of five.
- 300–500 million cases of malaria occur every year.
- Symptoms include fever, headache, repeated vomiting, convulsions, coma and, in severe cases, death.

**B** Malaria – the grim details

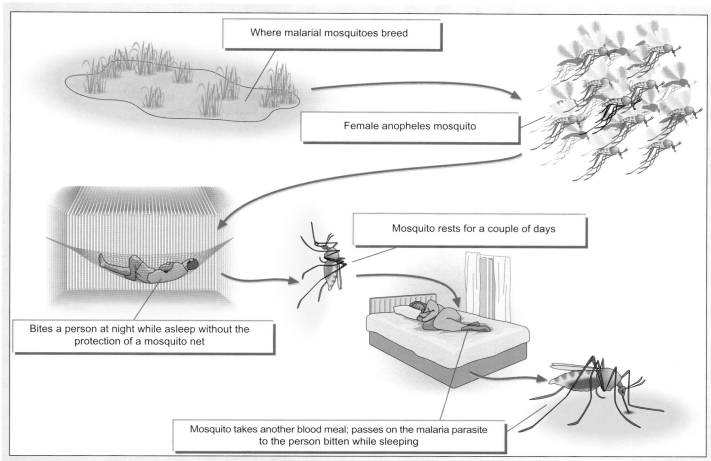

**C** How malaria spreads

Labels in diagram:
- Where malarial mosquitoes breed
- Female anopheles mosquito
- Mosquito rests for a couple of days
- Bites a person at night while asleep without the protection of a mosquito net
- Mosquito takes another blood meal; passes on the malaria parasite to the person bitten while sleeping

If hundreds of millions of people in the world are affected by malaria, why has no one found a cure for it? The parasite that causes malaria has shown a great ability to change and build resistance against the drugs used to fight it. Chloroquine was a cheap drug without side-effects, perfect for use in poor countries, but now in many parts of Africa resistance to the drug has reached 90 per cent. There are no other effective cheap drugs.

The big drug companies, based in the USA and Europe, are often accused of not spending enough money on looking for a vaccine against malaria because the disease does not affect people living in MEDCs. There is no money for drug companies in researching drugs for poor people! Will global warming, if it brings back malarial mosquitoes to southern Europe and USA, come to the rescue of people in LEDCs?

## Activities

**1** a) Name *three* diseases that occur more commonly in tropical countries than in the UK.

   b) Describe the link between water and diseases in the tropics.

**2** Why is malaria less of a problem in tropical areas with low densities of population?

**3** A charity is trying to persuade governments and drug countries to spend more on research into a vaccine against malaria. You have to write the report to show that malaria is a very serious disease needing urgent attention.

a) Think about headings to be used for the report. You could include: numbers affected, areas affected, bad effects on people, benefits if a successful vaccine is discovered.

b) Write the report and illustrate it with maps, graphs and diagrams where appropriate.

**4** Visit the UK government's website for health advice for travellers by using the Hotlinks site (see page 2). Explain what tourists to tropical countries can do to reduce the risk of catching malaria and other tropical diseases.

# Why are countries in sub-Saharan Africa poorest of all?

> Looking at the physical and human problems in Africa
> Understanding why these problems lead to poverty

Figure **A** on page 108 showed the great development divide between MEDCs and LEDCs. Table **A** below shows the gap between countries in sub-Saharan Africa and the average for all LEDCs. The gap is growing, especially in those African countries worst affected by HIV/AIDS. Life expectancy has fallen below 40 years in some countries. How many fewer people would you know if life expectancy in the UK was just 40 years? Families in Africa are losing their strongest workers on the land.

| Measure of development | Average for LEDCs | Sub-Saharan Africa |
|---|---|---|
| GDP per head (US $) | 2904 | 1377 |
| Life expectancy at birth (years) | 61 | 49 |
| Adult literacy rate (%) | 70 | 56 |
| % of people with access to safe water | 71 | 51 |

**A** How sub-Saharan Africa compares with other LEDCs

## WHY IS AFRICA THE CONTINENT OF POVERTY?

As is usually the case in geography, the reasons are a mixture of physical and human. Some of these are shown in map **B**.

### Physical difficulties

Much of Africa is dry – the Sahara is the world's largest desert. Rainfall is unreliable in the Sahel and in southern Africa; when the rains do not arrive, many areas are affected by drought. The east coast can be hit by tropical storms and heavy rains which cause the opposite problem – flooding over wide areas. Farmers in rich countries would find it difficult to cope with these climatic extremes. What chances have poor African farmers?

### Human problems

Wars and armed conflicts between different tribes are common. Most African countries are artificial creations: look at the number of straight-line borders on map **B**. European countries, mainly Britain, France, Portugal and Belgium, carved up the land between them as **colonies** and took no account of tribal boundaries. These colonies were created for the benefit of the European countries. Some African countries are badly governed by dictators and corrupt politicians who plunder their country's wealth and resources. Also, a lot of African countries suffer from huge debt: they borrowed money from the World Bank and paying it back allows the cycle of poverty to continue.

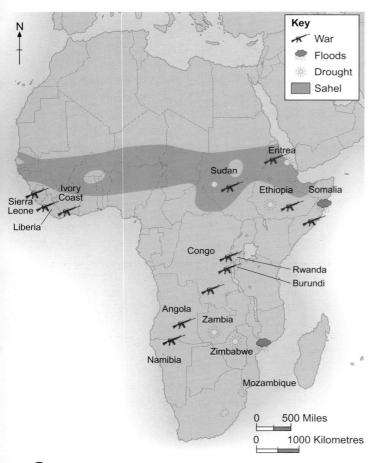

Key
- War
- Floods
- Drought
- Sahel

0    500 Miles
0    1000 Kilometres

**B** Physical and human crises in Africa

Africa's wealth lies in its **primary products** – minerals, tropical hardwoods and crops like cocoa. These were exported to Europe in raw form, which meant little value was added in Africa. The value was added in other countries when these primary products were made into **secondary products**. The same pattern of trade continues today, with African countries exporting their valuable natural resources for low prices (pages 116–117).

## FACT FILE     PROBLEMS IN THE COUNTRYSIDE

Figure **C** illustrates the traditional farming still practised in many parts of West Africa. Tribes keep mixed herds of animals that are taken to grazing land by day and brought back to the village compound at night. Dotted around the village are small fields of subsistence crops such as maize and millet. Fuel wood is collected from woodland close to the village. Waterholes in stream beds are often the only source of drinking water for both people and animals.

Pressure from population growth has led to the overuse of land and its destruction by **soil erosion**. As more trees are cleared for fuel and cultivation, more of the land surface is exposed to wind and rain. During droughts strong winds blow away the fertile topsoil. When the heavy tropical rains return, soil is washed away and the surface is cut into deep valleys.

 **Traditional pattern of farming by tribal groups in West Africa**

## Activities

Look at *SKILLS in geography*, pages 145–155 for help with these activities.

**1**   Use the information from table **A** to prove that sub-Saharan Africa is the world's poorest region.

**2**   a) Draw *two* spider diagrams for (i) physical reasons and (ii) human reasons for the poverty of African countries.

   b) Choose *one* reason from each diagram. Explain how each one contributes to poverty.

**3**   Look at **C** and describe the landscape and land uses in the area shown.

   a) How are living and farming here different from in the UK? List as many differences as you can.

   b) Draw a sketch to show what this area might look like in ten years' time after further increases in population. Explain the main differences you have shown on your sketch.

# Is world trade fair?

> Understanding why world trade is unfair to LEDCs
> Looking at how MEDCs can help make trade fairer for LEDCs

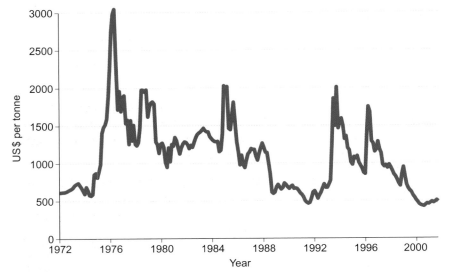

A  World coffee prices, 1972–2002

The scales of trade are tipped against LEDCs. Many LEDCs rely on the export of primary products, for example minerals, such as oil or iron ore, and foods, such as bananas, cocoa and coffee. These are low in value. MEDCs are more likely to export high-tech manufactured goods, which are high in value. Value is added when primary products are made into other goods (secondary products) in factories. The result is that, for example, farmers in LEDCs need to export a lot of coffee beans to pay for the import of one tractor.

There is another problem for LEDCs. World prices of raw materials fluctuate – they go up and down like a yo-yo. Coffee-growers and coffee-producing countries never know how much money they are going to make – or not going to make! Look at the world coffee prices shown in **A**. It was great to be a coffee-grower in 1975, unless they were in one of the areas affected by frost. Life was not as rosy in 2000 when prices touched a 30-year low.

## FACT FILE  COFFEE AND THE FAIR TRADE MOVEMENT

Coffee beans grow on bushes on coffee estates, often located on the mountainsides in tropical countries, such as Brazil, Colombia, Costa Rica and Kenya (see **B**). The ripe beans are picked, put in bags and shipped, mainly to North America and Europe where food and drink companies such as Nestlé roast the beans and put the processed coffee in jars for sale in shops. When you buy a jar of instant coffee for £2, how much goes to the coffee farm (**C**) that grew the beans? Take a guess.

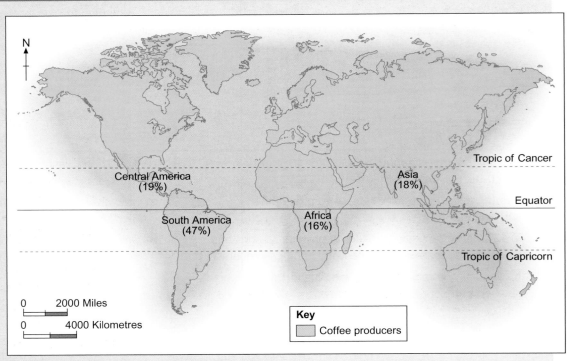

B  Coffee-producing areas – are they all in LEDCs?

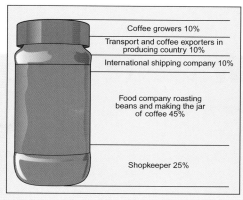

Coffee growers 10%

Transport and coffee exporters in producing country 10%

International shipping company 10%

Food company roasting beans and making the jar of coffee 45%

Shopkeeper 25%

**C** Coffee farm in the tropical regions of Central America, on the fertile lower slopes of a volcano

**D** Who makes the instant profit from a jar of coffee?

Look at **D** to find the answer – 20 pence at the most. What percentage of the final price remains in the coffee-growing country? Big companies responsible for shipping, roasting and selling the coffee are the ones that make the money. The majority are based in MEDCs. Therefore LEDCs gain at best 20 per cent of the £2 paid for a jar of instant coffee. The cut for MEDCs is 80 per cent. Is this an example of fair trade?

## The Fair Trade movement

You can follow the links on Hotlinks (see page 2) to find out about the Fair Trade movement. It began in 1993 to try to give small-scale farmers growing cocoa in LEDCs a fair price for their crops. Fair Trade guarantees growers a minimum price, even when world market prices fall, so that growers can keep on producing:

- World cocoa price falls to US $1000 per tonne
- Fair Trade guaranteed price is US $1600 per tonne.

On top of this, Fair Trade gives US $150 per tonne for community development projects, aimed at improving quality of life for all in the area, not just cocoa-growers. If the world market price for cocoa rises above US $1600, they receive the market price plus US$150 per tonne. Fair Trade now works for other crops, such as coffee, as well (see **E**).

Have you or your family ever bought a Fair Trade product? In UK supermarkets you can now buy Fair Trade chocolate, coffee, tea and fruit juices, among other products. They are more expensive but the price reflects what the farmers get for their hard work. The total market for Fair Trade products was worth £100m by 2004 in the UK, double the total for 2002, but still only a tiny ercentage of all food and drink sold. Nearly five million growers and their families in LEDCs are benefiting from the sale of Fair Trade goods.

**E** Fair Trade coffee – note the Fair Trade logo at the top left. Will the packaging attract shoppers?

## Activities

**S**

**1** Describe how graph **A** shows that:

a) world coffee prices fluctuate

b) prices are low in 2002.

Use values from the graph in your answers.

**2** Who gets what from the sale of a £1 bar of chocolate in the UK? The shop gets 33p; chocolate company 39.5p; government VAT 17.5p; transport and marketing in LEDC 6p; cocoa farmer 4p.

Draw a diagram, sketch or graph to show these amounts. Look at *SKILLS in geography* pages 145–155 if you need help.

**3** Explain why LEDCs consider that most world trade is unfair to them.

**4** Work in groups.

a) Design a questionnaire about buying Fair Trade products. Try to discover whether people in your class have bought Fair Trade goods, why or why not, and what will encourage them or stop them from buying them in the future.

b) Show the results and write about them. Were you surprised? Do people buy more or fewer Fair Trade goods than you thought?

**5** What do you think are the chances of an increase in Fair Trade? Give your reasons.

# What a difference clean water makes

> ## Looking at the links between clean water and quality of life in LEDCs

Did you know that every ten seconds a child somewhere in the world dies from diseases carried by dirty water? Can you imagine living in a village and getting your water from a contaminated stagnant pond or muddy stream – for drinking, bathing and washing clothes? This is what many villagers in rural areas of LEDCs have to do every day.

## FACT FILE    TAKING CLEAN WATER AND SANITATION TO RURAL AREAS IN PAKISTAN

The Punjab Rural Water Supply and Sanitation Project was funded with a loan from the ADB (Asian Development Bank). The aim was to provide a simple, low-cost, clean water supply and sanitation system to 800 000 people in over 300 villages, where monthly income per family is less than US $60. Under the scheme, safe water is piped to households from tube wells that tap into underground stores of uncontaminated water.

This project was one of the first to use a community-based approach. Village people were asked what they wanted. The clear message from the villagers was that they wanted to lead better lives – send their children to school, improve health and sanitation and increase income. A safe water supply was seen as the best start to achieve these aims.

 **A** Information about the Punjab in Pakistan

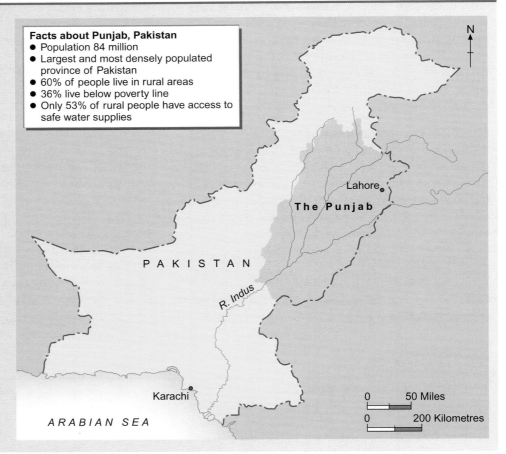

**Facts about Punjab, Pakistan**
- Population 84 million
- Largest and most densely populated province of Pakistan
- 60% of people live in rural areas
- 36% live below poverty line
- Only 53% of rural people have access to safe water supplies

## THE KNOCK-ON EFFECTS...

The story of Sughran Bibi, a mother of five, living in a cotton-growing region in the southern Punjab is typical. The scheme to pipe clean water to homes was completed here in 2001.

### Before
"We used to get our water from a pond also used by the animals. It was so dirty. Then they dug a well, but we had to queue all day under the sun to get a little water. The water wasn't good. Many children got sick with diarrhoea, and there was cholera in the rainy season. We had no money to go to the doctor. Life was so bad that some families left the village. My girls wanted to go to school but there was no time because we spent five to six hours a day fetching water. Mothers would say to their daughters: 'First you must fetch the water, then you can study!' ".

## After

"Life is much better now. I have time for sewing and embroidery. I make clothes that I sell. We don't have to skip meals any more. I have time to look after our home vegetable plot. My girls now go to school. They are hardly ever ill. I feel good because I am helping to bring money into the home. My dream has come true."

In the villages in this region, the knock-on benefits from having a piped clean water supply are significant. Water-related diseases have decreased by 90 per cent. School attendance has increased by 80 per cent. Household incomes have gone up by 20 per cent, mainly because women have more time to generate income by making clothes and keeping chickens, as well as taking goods to town markets to sell.

# SMALL-SCALE SCHEMES HELP LOCAL PEOPLE MOST

The Play-Pump is a South African invention that uses a children's roundabout to power a water pump (**B**, **C**). More than 400 have been installed, many of them near primary schools, which should not be a surprise. It is easy for local people to maintain because it uses low technology with only two moving parts. Advertising hoardings around the water tower are intended to provide enough revenue to pay for any repairs. One pump can draw up 1400 litres of water an hour from as much as 40 metres deep – more than enough for a village. This is better than piping and pumping water from a large dam hundreds of miles away.

**B** Play-Pump in a water playground in South Africa. Reproduced with permission of Roundabout (www.roundabout.co.za)

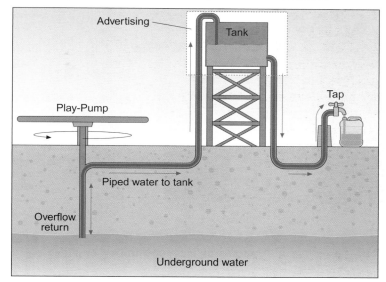

**C** Diagram showing how a Play-Pump works

## Activities

(S) (≣) (A)

1. Make *two* lists using the headings 'Quality of Life Before' and 'Quality of Life After' the clean water supply project for Sughran Bibi and other villagers. Then rank the information under the headings in order of importance.

2. In South African villages the Play-Pump has been a great success. Can you give *two* reasons for its success?

3. A charity is trying to raise money for water projects in LEDCs. You have been asked to write a report explaining why improved access to clean water supplies is so important to people in LEDCs.

   a) Look back through this chapter and make brief notes of information that might be used in the report (e.g. figures for percentage access to safe water in LEDCs and sub-Saharan Africa, effects of dirty water on health and poverty, and examples of the great improvements supplies of clean water can bring).

   b) Write the report.

# Are poor countries caught in a trade and poverty trap?

> Looking at examples of the poverty trap in LEDCs
> Making connections between different factors

**A** Prices of crops from tropical countries are high in UK shops

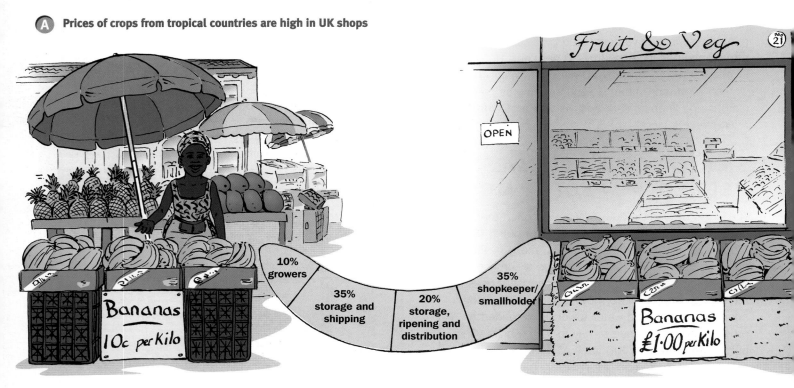

Fruit & Veg

OPEN

Bananas 10c per kilo

10% growers

35% storage and shipping

20% storage, ripening and distribution

35% shopkeeper/ smallholder

Bananas £1·00 per kilo

**B** Foreign exchange from exporting crops is a vital source of income for many poor tropical countries

**Caribbean farmer:**
'My country is too small and too poor to make tractors. All our tractors, trucks and other machines must be imported.'

**Government Minister in LEDC:**
'We need the money to pay off our debts. Having to sell cheap and buy dear has put the country in debt. The size of our debt keeps on increasing.'

**C** Finding other ways of earning foreign exchange is difficult

**Caribbean farmer:**
'I have spent a lot of money on my banana plantation. I cannot pull all the plants out now. Will any other crop give me more money?'

**Businessman in LEDC:**
'I am told that there is a big demand for sports gear in the USA. Wages are low here but clothes made here are blocked from the USA by high import taxes and quotas.'

**D** Persuading governments of MEDCs to give development aid is not easy

**Government Minister in MEDC:**
'We fund major schemes like dam building. They make a big difference to poor countries.'

**Charity worker:**
'Water and electricity from big dams go to the cities and rich people, not to the village people in greatest need.'

**E** Solutions using local resources and communities and low technology are often much more effective

**Villager in southern Africa:**
'The new biogas converter is amazing; it turns dung into methane gas for cooking and lighting. It used to take hours to collect enough wood.'

## Activities

**1**  Study mind map **F** showing why poor countries are caught in a trade and poverty trap. Describe and explain the links shown, then on a copy of the diagram add notes to explain the links.

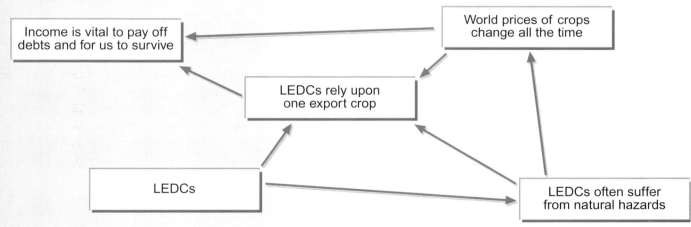

**F** Mind map

**2**  Study the information in **A**.

a)  Draw a pie graph to show how the money from selling a banana is divided up. Look at *SKILLS in geography* pages 145–155 if you need help.

b)  What percentages of the selling price go to LEDCs and MEDCs?

c)  Explain why this is an example of unfair trade.

d)  How would you make the trade fairer?

**3**  Using sources **B–E**, find *two* problems caused by poor countries being paid so little for their exports.

**4**  Using **A–E**, explain why it is very difficult for countries to get out of this trade trap.

# Rich country, poor country

1   Photographs **A** and **B** were taken in Peru, an LEDC in South America.
a) Which photograph shows high development? Explain your choice.
b) Which photograph shows low development? Explain your choice.

2   Work in small groups. Draw up a development plan for improving the life and farming for people in sub-Saharan Africa (SSA). Look back at the sources on pages 114–115 for information and ideas. Use the following as a guide:
a) How poor are the countries in SSA?
b) Why are these countries so poor?
c) Suggest a six-point plan to improve their way of life and farming. You could include solutions to the fuel and water problems.
d) Explain how your plan would improve the people's way of life and farming. Would anyone lose out?

Present your reports to the rest of the class. They can use the following mark scheme to give you an assessment of your work.

**Level 3**
- Makes some simple comparisons between SSA and other LEDCs
- Gives simple reasons why SSA is so poor
- A few suggestions made as to how it could be improved – five or less
- Uses some geographical words

**Level 4**
- Makes comparisons between SSA and other LEDCs
- Makes reference to different countries in the comparison
- Begins to recognise patterns, e.g. different areas that are richer or poorer
- Understands how the way of life could be improved – plan has several points that are explained
- Can offer their own views about how things will be improved

**Level 5**
- In addition, the report recognises that places and people are dependent upon others
- Shows some understanding of sustainability, i.e. that the suggested plan will bring lasting positive improvement
- Shows some ability to classify problems or solutions, e.g. into human and physical
- Shows some understanding of ideas such as the trade trap, poverty cycle and fair trade

**Level 6**
- In addition, the report recognises that places and people are dependent upon others
- Shows clear understanding of sustainability, i.e. that the suggested plan will bring lasting positive improvement
- Shows clear ability to classify problems or solutions, e.g. into human and physical
- Shows clear understanding of ideas such as the trade trap, poverty cycle and fair trade

**A** City wealth – part of Lima, the capital city, where rich people live

**B** Poverty in the countryside – a farming village in the Andes

# » 8   South and East Asia

Have you seen washing like this? This is Dhobi Ghats, Mumbai's main laundry where 5000 men work and beat the dirt out of sheets and clothes. A large, hard-working and cheap workforce is one of Asia's main assets. What would happen if these men were replaced by machines?

## *Learning objectives*

What are you going to learn about in this chapter?

> The major features of the physical and human geography of Asia
> The geography of Japan and the reasons for the country's great industrial importance
> South Korea's industrial growth and the problems it has caused
> How China, the world's population giant, is also trying to become an industrial giant
> The geography of the Indian sub-continent and the rise of hi-tech industries in India
> How Bangladesh struggles with its geography because of repeated flooding

 **A** Dhobi Ghats, Mumbai's **main laundry**

# Asia – the big continent

> Learning about the geography of Asia
> Comparing the climates of Asia and the UK

FACT FILE **THE GEOGRAPHY OF ASIA**

Everything about the physical geography of Asia is on a large scale.

- It is the largest continent, half as big again as Africa, the second largest.

- The Himalaya is the highest mountain range in the world, with thirteen peaks above 8000 metres, including Mount Everest. In no other continent does the highest mountain reach even 7000 metres above sea level (see **B**). Earth movements may still be pushing the Himalaya up even higher.

- Although the Amazon and Nile are longer than any Asian river, five of the world's ten longest rivers are in Asia. The Yangtze River, flowing through central China, is the longest in Asia but is still 315 km shorter than the Nile.

- The Caspian Sea is the world's largest lake.

- The land around the Dead Sea is the lowest on the Earth's surface (403 m below sea level).

- The Arabian and Gobi deserts are the second and third largest deserts. The Sahara, in Africa, is the largest.

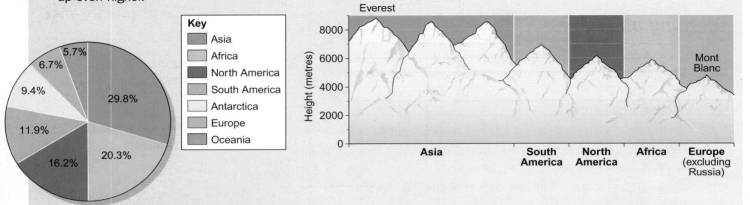

**Key**
- Asia
- Africa
- North America
- South America
- Antarctica
- Europe
- Oceania

5.7%
6.7%
9.4%
11.9%
16.2%
20.3%
29.8%

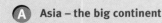

**A** Asia – the big continent

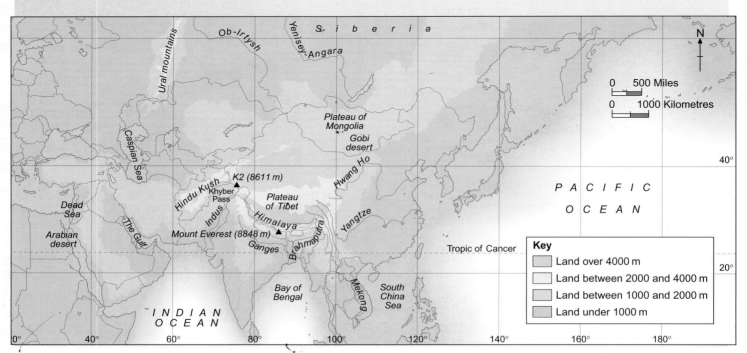

**Key**
- Land over 4000 m
- Land between 2000 and 4000 m
- Land between 1000 and 2000 m
- Land under 1000 m

**B** Physical map of Asia

# ASIA – CONTINENT OF CLIMATIC CONTRASTS

Asia stretches from south of the Equator (0°) to north of the Arctic Circle (66½°N). It is not surprising that there are large differences in weather and climate. Look at **C**. Singapore lies almost on the Equator and has a typical hot, wet Equatorial climate. Verkhoyansk is north of the Arctic Circle in Siberia. Which are the really big differences in temperature and precipitation between them?

One type of climate associated with Asia (especially India) is the tropical **monsoon**. For most of the year winds are dry because they blow from land to sea. Then in mid summer the wind direction changes: winds blowing from the sea bring heavy rain to India and neighbouring countries. These monsoon rains are vital for growing padi (wet rice); rice is the **staple crop** which feeds Asia's billions.

When monsoon winds bump into the hills of north eastern India and are forced to rise, water falls from clouds by the bucketful – literally. Cherrapunji (1300 metres above sea level) is the wettest place in the world with an average rainfall of 10 799 mm per year. It holds the world record for the amount of rain in a day – an estimated 900 mm.

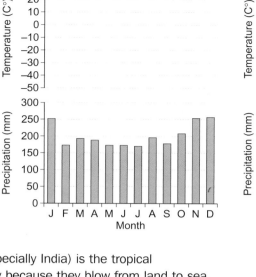
Singapore

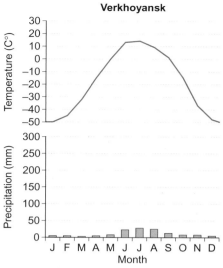
Verkhoyansk

 **Climates of Singapore and Verkhoyansk**

## SKILLS

**How to describe a climate graph**

Find the:
1 highest temperature and month
2 lowest temperature and month
3 range of temperature (highest minus lowest)
4 highest precipitation and month
5 lowest precipitation and month
6 precipitation distribution (all year, season with most).

*For more help* see page 148 of *SKILLS in geography*.

## Key words

**Monsoon** – climate with one season of heavy rainfall, as in India
**Staple crop** – the most important food in people's diets

## Activities

1 Use **B** to describe the following.
  a) The locations of Siberia, the Gobi desert and Plateau of Tibet.
  b) The courses followed by any two big Asian rivers.
  c) The use of colours to show differences in height.

2 a) Describe the differences in climate between Singapore and Verkhoyansk using the method suggested in the *SKILLS* box. Make a large table for your answers.
  b) (i) What are the two biggest differences in climate between them?
     (ii) Can you explain these differences?

3 a) The wettest part of England is the Lake District (see table below). Draw a rainfall graph to show the data.
  b) Use Hotlinks (see page 2) to look up rainfall data for your own region of the UK.
  c) (i) How does rainfall in the UK compare with that of Singapore?
     (ii) Does the UK have a wet climate? Look back to Chapter 5 before answering.

|     | J | F | M | A | M | J | J | A | S | O | N | D |
|-----|---|---|---|---|---|---|---|---|---|---|---|---|
| mm | 170 | 115 | 85 | 80 | 80 | 85 | 105 | 130 | 140 | 180 | 155 | 150 |

**Monthly precipitation in Keswick (total 1475 mm)**

# Asia – continent of many people

> Learning about the population of Asia

> Comparing the populations of Asia and other parts of the world

## FACT FILE  THE POPULATION OF ASIA

Four of the world's largest countries are in Asia: Russia, China, India, and Kazakhstan. Most of the land covered by Russia is east of the Urals in Asia, although Moscow, the capital city, is in the European part. These large countries cover great blocks of land, mainly in the dry and cold north and centre of Asia (see **A**). When compared to Russia and China, India seems quite small, but do not be fooled. India is as large as all of Western Europe. Notice how countries are smaller in south and east Asia, close to the Indian and Pacific Oceans. Indonesia, Philippines and Japan are countries composed of many islands.

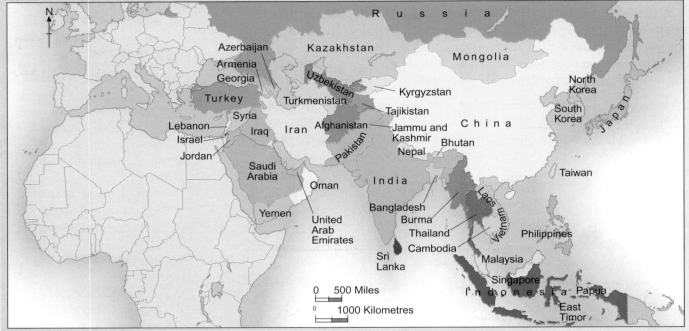

**A** Political map of Asia

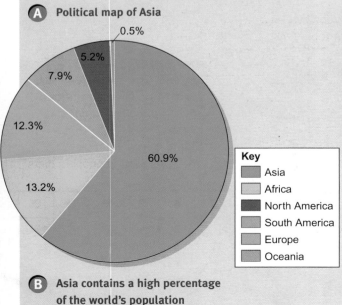

**Key**
- Asia
- Africa
- North America
- South America
- Europe
- Oceania

**B** Asia contains a high percentage of the world's population

| 1 | China | 1285.0 |
|---|---|---|
| 2 | India | 1025.1 |
| 3 | USA | 285.9 |
| 4 | Indonesia | 214.8 |
| 5 | Brazil | 172.6 |
| 6 | Pakistan | 145.0 |
| 7 | Russia | 144.7 |
| 8 | Bangladesh | 140.4 |
| 9 | Japan | 127.3 |
| 10 | Nigeria | 116.9 |

**C** The ten countries with the largest populations in 2001 (millions)

Even more impressive than country size is the huge number of people who inhabit Asia – not far short of three-quarters of the total world population (see **B** and **C**). More than one-third of the people in the world live in just two Asian countries, China and India. These countries are too large to be ignored by the rest of the world, particularly as both are undergoing dynamic economic growth (see pages 136–140).

# SOUTH AND EAST ASIA – DYNAMIC ECONOMIC GROWTH

Japan is now the world's second largest industrial country after the USA. In the past 30 years Japan has developed into a member of the rich club of MEDCs. This gave a lead that other Asian countries are determined to follow. Japan is sometimes described as 'the locomotive' that is hauling other Asian countries along the road of development (see Chapter 7 page 106).

The first to follow Japan's example were Hong Kong (**D**), Singapore, Taiwan and South Korea. These NICs (newly industrialising countries) became widely known as 'East Asian Tigers'. Why tigers? The *speed* of economic and industrial growth in the 1970s was nothing short of amazing. As traders, they were *strong* and *fierce*, willing to go out and sell *aggressively* in all world markets, even in the most competitive markets where *the law of the jungle* operated. They have since been joined by 'new tigers' such as Thailand, Indonesia, Malaysia and the Philippines.

At present Japan is the economic giant of Asia, but will it be overtaken by China and India within the next fifteen to twenty years?

**D** Hong Kong was one of the original East Asian Tigers before it was handed back to China in 1997; it has one of the world's great natural harbours

## Activities

**1** Study **A**.

a) Name Asian countries (*three* in total) with land both (i) north and south of the Equator (ii) on the mainland and on an island (iii) in Europe and in Asia.

b) Name *five* landlocked Asian countries (countries without a coastline). Try to give a reason why there are only a few of them.

**2** a) Draw either a pictograph or bar graph to show the estimates for 2050 in **E**. Highlight to show the Asian countries from the others.

b) Describe the main differences between the figures in **E** and those for 2001 in **C**.

**3** Study photograph **D**. Describe what it shows about the level of economic development in Hong Kong.

| 1 | India | 1 530 |
|---|---|---|
| 2 | China | 1 400 |
| 3 | USA | 400 |
| 4 | Pakistan | 350 |
| 5 | Indonesia | 300 |
| 6 | Nigeria | 260 |
| 7 | Bangladesh | 250 |
| 8 | Brazil | 240 |
| 9 | Ethiopia | 170 |
| 10 | Congo | 150 |

**E** Estimated sizes of the largest countries in 2050 (millions of people)

# Japan – geography and people

> **Understanding the geography of Japan**
> **Learning about traditional and western culture in Japan**

**A** Two quizzes about Japan

How much, if anything, do you know about the geography of Japan? Below there are two short quizzes. Try to answer the quiz questions before looking at the rest of the page.

### QUIZ 1

**JAPANESE GEOGRAPHY**

| | | | |
|---|---|---|---|
| Fuji | Hiroshima | Hokkaido | Honshu |
| Kyoto | Kobe | Kyushu | Narita | Osaka |
| Sapporo | Shikoku | Tokyo | Yokohama |

1  Name the largest island in Japan.
2  Which is the capital city?
3  Name the highest mountain.
4  Which was hit by a big earthquake in 1995?
5  Name the chief port.

### QUIZ 2

**JAPANESE COMPANIES AND BRAND NAMES**

| | | | | | |
|---|---|---|---|---|---|
| Canon | Fuji | Hitachi | JVC | Mazda | Minolta |
| Mitsubishi | NEC | Nikon | Nintendo | Nissan | Panasonic |
| Sharp | Sony | Subaru | Suzuki | Toyota | Yamaha |

1  Name a maker of play-stations and games.
2  Which company makes mobile phones?
3  Name one maker of TV sets.
4  Which company has a car factory in the UK?
5  Name one company that makes cameras.

Perhaps there was no contest, with geography the loser, no doubt! Nearly every household in the UK has some goods made by Japanese companies.

## FACT FILE   WHAT IS JAPAN REALLY LIKE?

Figure **B** gives basic geographical information. Japan is an island country (like the UK). The islands form a curve that extends for about 1900 km (1200 miles). Of the four big islands, Honshu is the largest and most important. Japan is in the temperate zone, although it lies further south than the UK, mainly between latitudes 30° and 45° north of the Equator (compared with 50°–60°N for the UK). The summer climate is hot and humid, especially in Tokyo and the south, and feels very uncomfortable. In autumn tropical cyclones, called typhoons in Japan, can strike the south coast (see page 110).

**Key**
Land over 500 m
● Major city
▲ Mountain

Sea of Japan

Sapporo
Hokkaido
Honshu
Japanese Alps
Kanto Plain
Kyoto
Tokyo
Yokohama
Hiroshima
Kobe
Nagoya
Kitakyushu
Inland Sea
Osaka
Mt. Fuji (3276 m)
Shikoku
Kyushu

PACIFIC OCEAN

0  100 Miles
0  200 Kilometres

45°
40°
35°

**B** Japan

Japan is a mountainous country; land above 500 metres covers more than 75 per cent of its area. The jagged peaks, rocky gorges, waterfalls and thick forests of the Japanese Alps provide splendid scenery. Mount Fuji (3276 m) is the highest peak (photo **C**). Flat coastal plains surround the mountains; the best farmland and most of the major cities are found here. Over 100 million people are squeezed into the lowlands. There is a great contrast between the densely populated plains, with their busy cities, and the sparsely populated mountainous interior, with its great natural beauty.

**C**  Mount Fuji, a perfect cone-shaped volcano

# A TRADITIONAL CULTURE IN A MODERN WORLD

Space is in such short supply in the cities that most families live in apartments that are tiny by UK standards. Most people sit on cushions on the floor and sleep on padded quilts called futons, which take up less space than chairs and beds in **western** homes. Not many people live in houses with gardens and garages. When land is needed for new projects, such as new airports for Osaka and Nagoya, it is created by **reclamation** of land from the sea.

Until recently almost all Japanese people lived in small villages, where life was hard and people had to cooperate with each other. In Japanese society the group is considered more important than the individual. The working day in many Japanese offices and factories begins with group exercise sessions and chanting of the company anthem.

First-time British visitors to Japan often notice these things.

- Japanese formality – everyone bows in shops, hotels and everywhere.
- Cities packed with people – crowds on the trains, in the streets, everywhere.
- Many school groups, all immaculately dressed in uniforms.

**D** Traditions survive longest in the countryside, where most people are rice farmers, growing some crops in terraced fields on the mountainsides

## The spread of Western culture

Western culture has spread to Japan and brought change, particularly among young people.

- Clothes – young Japanese follow western fashions and designs.
- Food – there is no longer rice with every meal; the young eat more meat, bread and dairy produce than their parents; McDonald's and other American diners are popular eating places.
- Sport – although martial arts (fighting without weapons, such as judo and karate) and sumo wrestling are still popular, baseball and football have passionate supporters. Large European clubs such as Manchester United and Real Madrid make pre-season tours because of the size of their Japanese fan clubs.

## Activities

1. Trace or draw a sketch map to show the main features of the physical geography of Japan.

2. What are the differences in Japan between a) mountain and plain and b) traditional and modern? Write *two* paragraphs to include at least *three* differences in each case.

3. **Postcard from Japan**

   a) Sketch a typical Japanese scene that could be used for a postcard.

   b) Write to a friend as if you were on a visit to Japan. Concentrate on describing the differences that visitors from the UK would notice. Use Hotlinks (see page 2) to find more information.

4. Find out what these words refer to. They are all related to Japan.

   a) shinkansen   b) kimono   c) origami   d) Shinto
   e) sake   f) sushi   g) yen

## Key words

**Reclamation** – making land useful for settlement or farming
**Terraced** – where level strips of land are cut out of hillsides
**Western** – lifestyles in Europe and North America as opposed to those in the East, mainly Asia

# Japan – industrial powerhouse of Asia

> Understanding Japan's industrial success
> Finding out which industries have grown in Japan

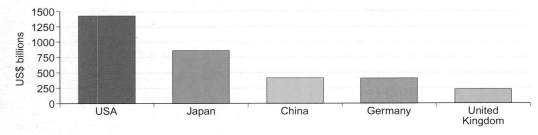

**A** Top five countries for manufacturing output in 2003

Japan is now Number Two in the world for manufacturing industrial goods (**A**). The remarkable industrial rise of Japan since 1950 has turned Japanese companies and brands into household names across the world. Why did it happen in a country without an industrial history and with few natural resources for industry?

## FACT FILE    INDUSTRIAL TAKE-OFF

The Japanese success story began with **heavy industries** such as steel, shipbuilding and chemicals. The Japanese copied and improved upon what the West was doing. For example, they built new, modern shipyards where ships were built faster and cheaper. Traditional shipbuilding areas in the UK, such as Tyneside, Glasgow and Belfast, were unable to compete. Shipyard closures speeded up in the 1970s and 1980s and shipbuilding almost disappeared in the UK.

The Japanese then started making **consumer goods** such as TVs, music systems, cars and cameras. Not only did they improve quality and reliability but they sold them at lower prices: an instant win for Japan and a loss for western companies. How did they do it?

One answer was greater use of machinery and robots on factory assembly lines (**B**). Japanese factories have some of the most advanced equipment in the world, because they invested some of their profits in new technology to keep ahead of competitors. In the best Japanese tradition, companies also looked after their workers, some of the most loyal and skilled in the world.

### Technology take-off

Times were hard for Japanese makers of electronics goods in the 1990s. The country's manufacturing costs were higher than those in neighbouring countries like South Korea and China. So they decided to spend lots of money researching a new technology, and now Japan is the world leader in **digital technology**. At least 70 per cent of all the digital consumer products sold in the world in early 2005 were manufactured in Japan by Japanese companies. This is an astonishing domination of such a large and rapidly growing market.

**B** Car assembly in Japan, where the emphasis is on quality, reliability and value for money

Across the world consumers are trading in and switching from:

- cameras with film to digital cameras
- analogue TVs with their bulky cathode-ray tubes to LCD or plasma flat-panel screens
- VCRs to DVD recorders
- fixed-line phones to Internet-enabled mobiles with a colour-screen camera facility.

# THE CROWDED SOUTHERN COAST OF HONSHU

Almost half of Japan's population lives in the coastal belt from Kobe to Tokyo (C). This is a huge conurbation stretching for over 300 km (200 miles) along the Pacific Coast, linking together Japan's four largest cities. This area is home to most Japanese industries. Newer consumer industries such as cars and electronics compete for land with longer established heavy industries like steel, shipbuilding, chemicals and oil-refining.

The Kanto plain in Central Honshu is the largest lowland area in Japan. The Tokyo **metropolitan** area, which includes the port city of Yokohama and the industrial city of Kawasaki, is the world's biggest city with about 27 million people. (London has eight million people.) The prosperity of Japan can be seen everywhere:

- clusters of modern skyscrapers in the business districts
- streets lined with glittering high-rise buildings that house fashionable department stores, elegant shops and expensive apartments
- roads filled with expensive, latest-model cars.

 Tokyo – a bustling modern city, full of traffic and people

## Activities

1. a) Describe what graph **A** shows about Japan and the UK as industrial countries.
   b) Give *two* reasons why Japan is a more successful industrial country today than the UK.
2. a) (i) Which digital goods do you and your family own?
      (ii) Look at the brand names – how many are made by Japanese companies?
   b) Explain why Japan is benefiting most as the world changes to digital.
3. a) Make a frame and draw a sketch of Tokyo from photo **C**.
   b) Label the features that show that it is a modern and prosperous city.
4. a) Use all four pages of information about Japan. Make a table and write into it the physical and human evidence to show that shortage of space is a problem in Japan.
   b) Explain why it is such a big problem.

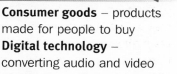

**Key words**

**Consumer goods** – products made for people to buy

**Digital technology** – converting audio and video signals into a form that can be processed by computers and accurately reproduced (through the use of numbers, i.e. digits)

**Heavy industries** – making large or bulky products such as ships and steel girders

**Metropolitan** – built-up area around the main city

# South Korea – country of chaebols

> Finding out what a chaebol is
> Investigating the link between chaebols and pollution in South Korea

Most people have never heard of chaebols, but nearly everyone has heard of at least one of these Korean companies: Samsung (**A, B**), LG (Lucky Goldstar), Hyundai, Daewoo. These are chaebols, companies controlled by Korean families that dominate economic activity in South Korea. They are huge multi-national companies that produce a wide range of goods, everything from ships and steel to cars and electronic goods.

**A** Samsung's head office in Seoul; Samsung is now four times larger than LG, its nearest rival chaebol

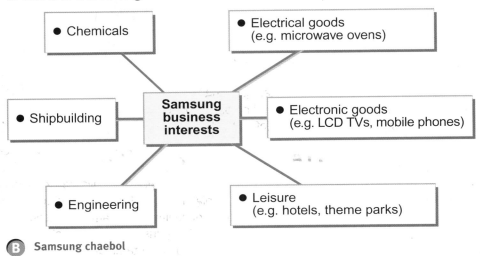

- Chemicals
- Electrical goods (e.g. microwave ovens)
- Shipbuilding
- **Samsung business interests**
- Electronic goods (e.g. LCD TVs, mobile phones)
- Engineering
- Leisure (e.g. hotels, theme parks)

**B** Samsung chaebol

## THE KOREAN MIRACLE

Until 1948 Korea was one country. Now it is split along the line of latitude 38°N. In North Korea the communist government does not encourage the growth of consumer industries. The story is very different in South Korea.

Dramatic change in South Korea began in the mid 1960s. Up to then it was a backward farming country, poor in natural resources. Today it is a dynamic industrial country, exporting everything from ships to the latest high-tech goods to markets worldwide. It is truly ambitious, always trying to match the industrial achievements of Japan.

What made the Korean miracle possible?

- Wages in South Korea were some of the lowest in the world.
- Koreans worked some of the world's longest hours.
- With no trade unions, they worked in some of the world's least safe working conditions, which kept costs down for factory-owners.
- The government placed high customs duties on the import of manufactured goods. It also encouraged Koreans to move from farms into the cities to provide a big pool of labour.
- Geography – Korea faces the Pacific, allowing easy export of manufactured goods by container ship to richer markets in Japan and the USA.

# CAN THE MIRACLE LAST?

By 1990 many workers felt that their bosses had exploited them for too long and there were widespread strikes and demonstrations against low wages and dreadful working conditions. As a result, South Korea is no longer a very low-cost producer of consumer goods. Competition from China increases every year, and the chaebols are facing challenging times.

Samsung has been forced to switch out of cheap electronic goods to concentrate on high-technology digital goods with higher profit margins. The two most important consumer items for Samsung in 2004 were:

- LCD (Liquid Crystal Display) flat-panel TVs
- Mobile phones – Internet-enabled with colour-screen cameras.

Samsung is one of the world's fastest growing technology companies. In 2004 it was the world's third largest maker of mobile phones, just behind Motorola (of Japan), but still well behind Nokia (of Finland).

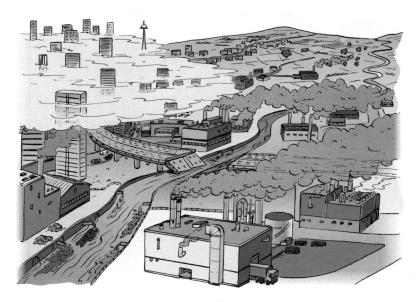

**C** South Korea after its Industrial Revolution

# ENVIRONMENTAL AND OTHER PROBLEMS

South Korean factory-owners, motivated by profits and growth, have never shown much interest in the environment. The air in big cities like Seoul is polluted by traffic and industrial fumes, causing breathing difficulties and damaging people's health. Rivers have died as they have filled up with industrial and domestic waste. The western part of the Yellow Sea is seriously contaminated.

Worries grew over quality of production when it was discovered that construction faults caused the collapse of a motorway bridge in 1994 (killing 32 people) and the Sampong shopping mall in Seoul in 1995 (killing 500). Some South Koreans began to ask: 'Has quality been sacrificed in the rush for rapid growth?'

|  | 1960 | 2000 |
|---|---|---|
| Agriculture | 62 | 10 |
| Industry | 10 | 28 |
| Services | 28 | 62 |

**D** Employment structure in South Korea (percentages)

## Activities

Look at pages 145–155 of *SKILLS in geography* if you need help.

**1**  a) Use table **D** to draw pie graphs for 1960 and 2000.

   b) Finish these two sentences.

   (i) The data shows growth in manufacturing industry because ...

   (ii) People working in agriculture are likely to be poor in South Korea because ...

**2**  How did a) labour, b) markets and c) government contribute to the growth of manufacturing industry in South Korea?

**3**  Draw a mind map. Put the words 'industrial growth' in the centre and then show the advantages of industrial growth for the Korean people and disadvantages for the environment.

**4**  Work in groups.

   a) **Brainstorm:** look at **C** and suggest ways to reduce pollution and clean up the environment in newly industrialising countries.

   b) Draw posters (i) to educate people and (ii) to show what places could look like after pollution control and clean-up.

# China – geography and history of development

> Understanding the geography of China
> Finding out why China is not like Japan and Korea

## FACT FILE    CHINA

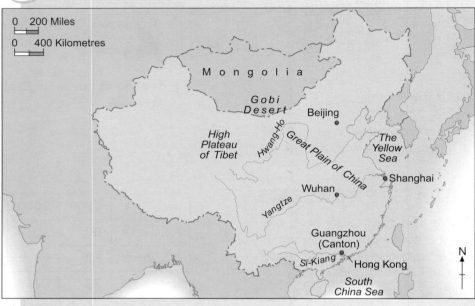

0   200 Miles

0   400 Kilometres

Mongolia

Gobi Desert

Beijing

High Plateau of Tibet

Hwang-Ho

Great Plain of China

The Yellow Sea

Shanghai

Wuhan

Yangtze

Guangzhou (Canton)

Si-Kiang

Hong Kong

South China Sea

N

**A** China

China is a huge country covering more than one-fifth of Asia. In terms of its physical geography, the country has everything – towering mountain peaks above 7000 metres high (Himalaya), high plateau (Tibet), desert (Gobi), big rivers (Yangtze and Hwang-Ho) and wide plains (Great Plain of China). Along its northern border are the Gobi Desert, Mongolia and Siberia; in the west are the Himalaya and Plateau of Tibet. All of them sound like places where few people live; not many do.

China has sometimes been called the 'land of the three rivers' – Hwang-Ho or Yellow River in the north, Yangtze in the centre and Si-kiang in the south. The majority of Chinese people live along the lower courses of these rivers, in the eastern third of the country. The rivers' floodplains provide wonderful growing conditions for the staple foods of wheat in the north (made into noodles and bread) and rice in the centre and south. Agriculture still dominates in China:

- 74 per cent of Chinese people live in villages in the countryside
- 60 per cent of Chinese workers are farmers.

Despite the importance of farming, there are over 100 cities with more than one million inhabitants in China. This compares with two in the UK (London and Birmingham). All the big cities are in the east. The capital Beijing is in the north east. The main port, centre of business and largest city is Shanghai at the mouth of the Yangtze in the middle. Guangzhou (formerly known as Canton) is the major industrial centre in the south east.

### Typical house
- Built of mud bricks, clay bricks or stone; roof made of tiles or straw; three or four rooms.

### Services
- Most have electricity except in remote areas, but few have piped water in the house.

### Possessions
- Many own a bicycle, radio and sewing machine.
- Fewer people than in cities have a TV set, washing machine or motor scooter.

### Daily life
- Work many hours per day, especially at busy times like planting and harvesting.
- Attend political meetings and night classes, where they learn how to read and write and how to use improved methods of farming.
- Have little time for recreation.

**B**  Village life in rural China

# A HISTORY OF SLOW ECONOMIC GROWTH

Why has China not become the economic superpower that its size and population would suggest? History offers an answer. Chinese civilisation is one of the world's oldest, having originated in the Yellow River basin some 5000 years ago. They have always tried to keep their civilisation intact. The 5000 km long Great Wall of China (see **C**) was built to keep out Mongol hordes from the north. Traders from Europe in the eighteenth and nineteenth centuries were made equally unwelcome.

**C** Part of the Great Wall of China, one of the human wonders of the world; building began as early as the third century BC

After the Communist Revolution in China in 1949, the State took control of all farming and industry. There was a big growth in industry, although these were mainly heavy industries like steel and chemicals. However, for the first 30 years the communist government blocked trade with western countries.

Then in 1979 the communist government changed its mind and allowed investment from overseas for the first time. This led to well known multi-nationals such as VW cars and Pepsi-Cola setting up factories in China in the 1980s. Since 1995 economic growth in China has been spectacular, with its GDP increasing at double the world average (see **D**).

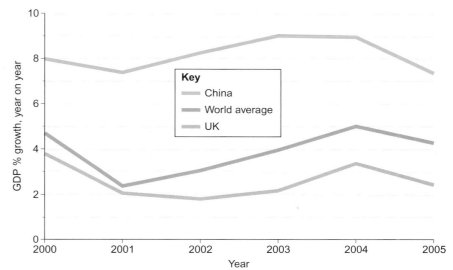

**Key**
- China
- World average
- UK

*GDP % growth, year on year* (vertical axis)
*Year* (horizontal axis)

**D** GDP percentage growth, 2000–5

## Activities

1 Try to give reasons for the following.

   a) The highest densities of population in China are in river valleys.

   b) Fewer than 10 per cent of Chinese people live in the north and west.

   c) Before 1979 economic growth in China was slow.

2 Use the dates given in the text to draw a time column for China from 1945 to 2005 (see the *SKILLS* box).

3 Look back at photo **B** on Chapter 7 page 122. Does the standard of living appear to be the same, higher or lower in China than in the Andes of Peru? Give your opinion and explain your answer.

4 Work in groups.

   a) Discuss the mental images group members have of China and of empty areas like the Himalaya, Gobi Desert and Mongolia.

   b) Trace or draw an outline map of China.

   c) Show these images on the map to make a mental map. Look at *SKILLS in geography* pages 145–155 for help with this.

### SKILLS

**How to make a time column**

1 Make a scale of dates down the side of the page.

2 Write in what happened at key dates.

3 Use } for a block of dates and write in what happened.

*For more help* see page 155 of *SKILLS in geography*.

# China – the giant stirs

> **Understanding manufacturing in China**
> **Finding out how this affects the rest of the world**

Although the numbers of privately owned businesses have increased dramatically since 1979, industry in China is still largely owned by the State. The government operates the large industrial plants, banks, transport and other services. Unlike Japan and Korea, Chinese company names are not well known in the west.

China's leaders recognised that they needed help from foreign companies to modernise the country's factories, improve scientific and technical training and get rid of waste and inefficiency.

## FACT FILE    MANUFACTURING IN CHINA

Manufacturing is growing by 5–10 per cent each year. China is now the third largest manufacturing country after the USA and Japan (see **A** on page 130). China is already responsible for 7 per cent of global manufacturing industry; some people think that this will reach 25 per cent by 2025.

### Reasons for this spectacular growth
Companies in the USA, Japan and Europe all want to invest in China. Think of all the things on sale in the UK with 'Made in China' written on them – pencils, calculators, electrical goods, sportswear, Christmas crackers … can you add to the list? Why does everyone want to set up factories, offices and stores in China?

Reason number 1 is low **costs of production**. Wages are low, while at the same time there is no shortage of Chinese workers. More than 300 million Chinese have migrated to the cities, providing a great pool of industrial workers.

Reason number 2 is **market**, both present and future. Chinese people living in the cities are becoming better off, so the Chinese market for consumer goods is rising. With one-fifth of the world's population, can any big company afford *not* to have a presence in China? VW sold more cars in China in 2003 than it did in Germany. B&Q's largest store is in Shanghai.

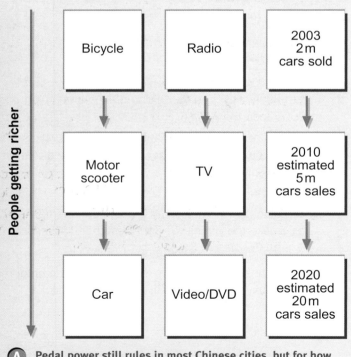

People getting richer

| Bicycle | Radio | 2003 2m cars sold |
| Motor scooter | TV | 2010 estimated 5m cars sales |
| Car | Video/DVD | 2020 estimated 20m cars sales |

**A** Pedal power still rules in most Chinese cities, but for how much longer?

# THE CONSEQUENCES OF CHINA'S GROWTH

## 1 Scrap prices at record levels in UK
- Prices doubled for many types of scrap in 2003–4.
- China was taking all that was collected for steel-making in China for use in its other industries. Even disused cars in the UK were worth £70 by the middle of 2004.

## 2 Growth in demand for oil and other minerals/metals
- World market prices at record levels in 2004 for oil and copper.
- China is power-hungry because of its fast-growing economy.

## 3 Dynamic cities
- Coastal manufacturing centres are richer than they have ever been. The results of spectacular progress can be seen best in Shanghai, the great trading and industrial city at the mouth of the Yangtze River.

## 4 Poverty in the countryside
- There is a widening gap between rich cities and poor villages.
- City incomes are on average three times higher than rural ones.
- One in eleven rural residents subsists on less than 637 yuan (about £40) per year.
- The expected trickle-down of wealth from city to countryside is not happening.

## 5 Pollution in the cities
- A World Bank survey shows that sixteen of the world's twenty most polluted cities are in China.
- Haze and smog caused by low-grade petrol used in cars are worst in Beijing.
- Doctors blame smog for sharp rises in cases of bronchitis and lung cancer.

## Activities

1. Why are large companies from all over the world rushing to set up businesses in China?

2. a) Make a list of differences between rural and urban areas in China.

   b) The Chinese government is worried about the growing gap between city and countryside. Can you suggest any reasons for the widening gap between them?

3. Work in pairs or small groups.

   a) **Brainstorming session:** note down costs and benefits resulting from the recent spectacular growth of industry in China using two headings: (i) China itself and (ii) other world countries. Think of as many as you can.

   b) As a class, rank the benefits and disadvantages in order from greatest impact to least impact on China and on other countries.

   c) In your own opinion, are the benefits to China greater than the costs? Explain your opinion to your neighbour. Do they have a different opinion? Try to persuade them to change their minds.

**B** Shanghai – does it look any different from an American or European city?

### Key words

**Costs of production** – amount of money needed to make something

**Dynamic cities** – urban areas changing fast due to rapid economic growth

**Market** – place where goods are sold

# The sub-continent – India, Pakistan and Bangladesh

> ### Understanding the geography of India, Pakistan and Bangladesh

**1 Himalayan mountains** leading into the Hindu Kush range in the north west – a great natural barrier with peaks more than 8 km high. At the top, the mountains are an uninhabitable world of snow, ice and bare rock. Routes through this formidable mountain barrier are few and far between; one of the best known is the Khyber Pass (see **B**).

Why were the countries of Pakistan and Bangladesh created? In the years leading up to 1947 this vast area was part of the British Empire. India was ruled as one country, despite being 30 times the size of Great Britain and having ten times its population and people with many different religions and languages.

## PHYSICAL GEOGRAPHY

The sub-continent splits neatly into three natural regions (see **A**). The one that is most important for its people, the Great Plain, stretches across all three countries.

**2 The great plain of the Indus and Ganges** stretching for almost 3000 km (2000 miles) through Pakistan, India and Bangladesh – covered by fertile silt. Up to 300 km (200 miles) wide, it is the most densely populated region; in all three countries, a majority of people live in villages and work on farms.

**3 The Deccan plateau** in peninsular India – a large triangular area of land. Mountain ranges border its eastern and western sides before the land drops down to coastal plains next to the Indian Ocean. Shortage of water is a problem in some parts. Population densities vary greatly from high to low.

**B** The Khyber Pass links Afghanistan and Pakistan; it has been important for trade between the West (Europe) and the East (India and Far East) for centuries

**A** Natural regions

# HUMAN GEOGRAPHY

Although India is much larger than the other two, there are many similarities between the three countries (table **C**). Can you see any evidence in the table that India is the best developed? They are, and will remain, three of the world's most populous countries (see pages 126 and 127). Streets and trains are always full of people (photo **D**).

Religion is very important in all three countries. It affects all aspects of daily life. When British rule in India ended in 1947, Pakistan was created as a separate country for Muslims. Muslims did not want to be ruled by the Hindu majority in India. Unfortunately the two largest Muslim groups lived 1000 miles apart in the new Pakistan. Apart from religion, the two parts had nothing in common. Differences in race, language and culture led to another split in 1971, between West Pakistan which became Pakistan, where Urdu is the main language, and East Pakistan which became Bangladesh – land of Bengali-speaking people.

Relations between the governments of India and Pakistan have never been good. Disputes continue over who owns Kashmir. When India and Pakistan play each other at cricket, which is the number one sport in both countries, rivalry is intense. Every match is played as if it were a cup final.

|  | India | Pakistan | Bangladesh |
|---|---|---|---|
| Total population (millions) | 1025 | 145 | 140 |
| Population density | 312 | 180 | 975 |
| Population growth (% per year) | 1.5 | 2.4 | 2.0 |
| GDP per head (US $) | 470 | 400 | 330 |
| Life expectancy (years) | 64 | 61 | 61 |
| Adult literacy (%) | 58 | 44 | 35 |
| Trade (US $ billions): | | | |
|    Value of exports | 44.0 | 8.5 | 6.0 |
|    Value of imports | 50.1 | 9.3 | 9.4 |
| Main export | Textiles and clothing | Textiles and clothing | Textiles and clothing |
| Main import | Crude oil and oil products | Machinery | Machinery |

**C** Country profiles (2003)

**D** Suburban shopping area and train in Mumbai, India's largest city

## Activities

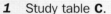

1 Study table **C**.

  a) Draw bar graphs to show the values for imports and exports in the three countries.

  b) Work out the size of the **trade gap** in each country.

  c) Make lists of the main similarities and differences between the three countries.

  d) What is the evidence that India is the best developed of the three?

2 a) Describe fully what the photographs in **D** show.

  b) Draw a sketch or find a photo showing a suburban shopping area in a UK city. Add labels to highlight the differences between the UK and India.

3 Look at the result from the 2001 Census below. It was for one of India, Pakistan or Bangladesh.

Hindus 80.2 per cent    Muslims 13.4 per cent
Others 6.4 per cent

  a) Draw a pie graph to show this data.

  b) Which country was it for? Explain your answer.

**Key word**

**Trade gap** – the difference between the value of imports and exports in any country

# Old India awakes

> **Finding out how India is becoming competitive in the world market**
> **Discovering what problems this has caused for India**

Until 1990 India appeared to be missing out on the Asian industrial boom, weighed down by:

- poor quality and outdated products
- no welcome for companies from outside India.

Attitudes have changed since 1991, led by the success at producing computer software and in attracting service jobs from overseas companies. India has enjoyed fifteen years of strong economic growth.

## INDIA CALLING

It's a dream job for Aditi Ekbote answering calls from HSBC customers. She has been at the bank's Hyderabad call centre for seven months... Aditi, 20, lives about 30 minutes from the call centre. She says, 'I dreamed about coming to work here since I was at university. My sister Poonam was already here and I saw what a good job it was.'...

Aditi works an eight-and-a-half hour shift including breaks... [She] earns about £2000 a year, but also has health insurance and is in the HSBC provident fund, the equivalent of a pension scheme. The bank also provides transport for staff to and from their homes.

**A** View from a call centre in Hyderabad, central India. Reproduced from *The Mail on Sunday*, 22 February 2004

Barely a day goes by without UK newspaper headlines such as 'RSA exports 1200 jobs to India'. RSA is one of the big insurance companies that, along with banks, airlines, credit card and telephone companies, are moving operations to Indian cities. Taking into account all the costs of training and recruiting staff, and operating the phone and computer links, UK companies estimate that their Indian operations are 40–50 per cent cheaper than UK ones.

'Differences in labour costs are crucial. In 2004 average wage costs including benefits for a call centre worker in the UK are £16 800, compared with £2300 in India and £4200 in Malaysia.'

'India is a highly educated country. It turns out two million graduates a year and most of them speak English. Workers in UK call centres are educated to A level at best.'

Each new phone job in India is reckoned to create another support job in the service sector, such as driving, catering or cleaning. Not all of the work exported is call centre work; some is in software programming and support, particularly in centres of IT like Bangalore. Jobs are much sought after and are seen as opportunities for learning new skills.

## BANGALORE – THE SILICON VALLEY OF INDIA

This southern city of six million people is the IT centre of India. It all began in 1984 when Texas Instruments set up a successful design centre here. Other multi-nationals and India's home-grown software companies followed. Home to more than 250 high-technology companies, the city is booming and has doubled in population during the past fifteen years. Something like 60 per cent of India's growing software exports come from Bangalore.

Most IT companies are located on the vast new technology parks that have sprung up around the city. Best known is Electronics City (photo **B**), which houses a mixture of international companies (such as Siemens and Digital) and Indian companies (Infosys and Velankani). It was built for companies who deal in information technology, software development, telecommunications, financial services and what are described as 'other non-polluting hi-tech industries'.

**B** Electronics City on the southern side of Bangalore

**C** Peenya Industrial Park

Many of Bangalore's longer established textile and engineering companies are located at Peenya Industrial Park (see **C**). Why do new hi-tech industries not use it?

Public services in the city have not been able to keep pace with the massive rise in business interests, which has led to many of the usual urban problems. Clogged roads, regular power cuts and water shortages are just three of the problems that need urgent attention if Bangalore's reputation as India's most go-ahead city is to be maintained. Many people have no choice but to build their own shelters (**D**).

**D** 'Homes' of new arrivals on the edge of Electronics City

## Activities

**1** State *two* reasons why some UK companies are transferring jobs to India.

**2** Make a list of the advantages of new call-centre jobs for India.

**3** List some of the disadvantages affecting India's quick growth.

**4** a) Make a table to show the differences between Electronics City (**B**) and older industrial parks (**C**) in Bangalore. Use these two headings:

   **(i)** What the buildings look like    **(ii)** What the area around the buildings looks like

  b) Why do hi-tech companies choose to locate in Electronics City instead of Peenya Industrial Park? You are the head of a computer chip company. Which industrial park would you choose? Can you explain why?

**5** Design a poster advertising the attractions of Electronics City in Bangalore for new companies. Think about your audience. Who is the poster aimed at? Make sure you choose the right sorts of images and words to appeal to them. Use Hotlinks (see page 2) to find out more about IT in Bangalore.

**6** Look at the comments in **E** about companies moving to India.

  a) Think about the comments one at a time. What is each person trying to say? Why is he/she saying it?

  b) Do you think people in the UK should be worried? Explain.

  c) Draw an opinion line like the one below and place the people along it where you think they should go. Now add yourself to the line and explain why you put yourself there.

FOR _____ AGAINST

> **Businesswoman:**
> 'There are 800 000 call centre jobs in the UK. The estimate for India is 60–80 000.'

> **Trade Union leader:**
> '200 000 UK jobs in banking and insurance could go by 2008.'

> **Labour MP:**
> 'This is a drip, drip process. People in my constituency are extremely worried about the future of business in the town.'

**E** Comments made in the UK in 2003

# Bangladesh – struggling with its geography

> Finding out about Bangladesh's unique geography
> Understanding the advantages and disadvantages of its geography

Bangladesh is one of the world's poorest countries. Its geography is dominated by its position on a delta. Two great rivers, the Ganges and the Brahmaputra, split up into many channels before entering the sea. They flow across a wide area of flat land, forming the world's largest river delta.

## What is *good* about living on a delta?

The quick answer is very fertile silt soils. Every time the rivers flood another layer of silt is deposited and soil fertility is renewed. All the land is flat and water is plentiful. Padi rice (the staple food) and jute (an export crop used for sacking and for backing on carpets) thrive in these conditions. Seventy-five per cent of Bangladeshis live in the countryside, and over 60 per cent of the country's workers are farmers.

## What is *bad* about delta living?

Rivers, lakes and swamps cover 10 per cent of the land area. More than half the country is less than one metre above sea level. Flooding is a regular natural event in every delta, but the risk is increased in Bangladesh because of its monsoon climate and frequent visits from cyclones. Both can bring enormous amounts of rainwater. Dhaka, the capital, expects to receive 437 mm in its wettest month (July), which is not much less than the London average for the whole year (593 mm). In September 2004 Dhaka had its worst rains for 50 years, with 350 mm falling in 24 hours on 13 September.

---

### FACT FILE   FLOODING IN BANGLADESH, 2004

## The flood that sank a nation

The people of Bangladesh used to expect the mighty Brahmaputra River to overflow about every 20 years, bringing death and destruction in its wake.

Then came a 1960s master plan for flood prevention... millions of pounds [of] aid were pumped into massive engineering projects. The depressing result was that the floods came even faster.

The gap between big floods shortened to 14 years, then 10 years and... 6 years after the devastating floods in 1998, much of Bangladesh is under water again.

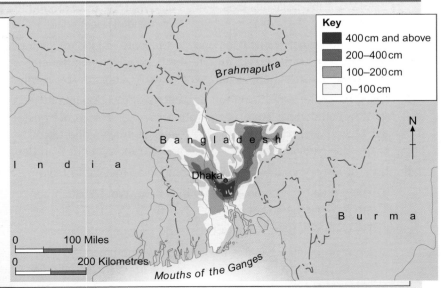

**A** Adapted from a newspaper report by Leonard Doyle, *The Independent*, 28 July 2004. © *The Independent* (2004)

**B** Devastating floods in 2004 – depth of flood water

- Floods covered half of Bangladesh, killing more than 760 people, directly affecting more than 35 million
- An estimated 8.5m homes were destroyed
- More than a million children are at risk of illness or death due to acute malnutrition within the next two months without more intervention, according to UN
- Worst rain in Dhaka for 50 years, with 35 cm falling in 24 hours on September 13
- Dhaka government puts cost of repairs to roads, agriculture and industry at $6bn (£3.3bn); World Bank estimate is $2bn
- Rice crops, fish farming and salt production badly affected
- World food programme distributing high-energy biscuits daily for next 10 months to 80,000 children in worst-hit districts.

**C** Flood facts, September 2004. Newspaper report by Lucy Ward, *Guardian*, 29 September 2004.
© Guardian Newspapers Limited (2004)

# Activities

| J | F | M | A | M | J | J | A | S | O | N | D |
|---|---|---|---|---|---|---|---|---|---|---|---|
| 18 | 31 | 58 | 103 | 194 | 321 | 437 | 305 | 254 | 169 | 28 | 2 |

**D** Average monthly rainfall in Dhaka (mm)

**1** a) Show the rainfall data for Dhaka in **D** on a bar graph.

b) When is the risk of flooding (i) highest and (ii) lowest? Give reasons for your answers.

**2** Make a table like the one below, but leaving much more space in the last two columns for answering. Fill it in using information from **A** and **C** on pages 138–139 and these two pages.

| Statement about Bangladesh | Information supporting it | Explanation |
|---|---|---|
| A One of the world's poorest countries | | |
| B Overcrowded and short of land | | |
| C Increasing risk of flooding | | |

**3** Carry out a short case study of the 2004 flood in Bangladesh. Include the following: sketch map of areas affected, causes of the flooding, effects on the Bangladeshi people, economic effects on Bangladesh.

**4** Study the comments in **E**.

a) Describe how the comments are different.

b) Suggest reasons why they are different.

c) Do you agree or disagree with them. Why?

**Government Minister:**
'Bangladesh is water and water is Bangladesh: floods are nothing new to us.'

**Bangladeshi newspaper against the government:**
'Flood control projects remain unfinished due to corruption. Builders bribe politicians to build blocks of flats and shopping plazas on waterways used for flood water.'

**Overseas expert on flood control:**
'The flooding can never be stopped. The real problem is a population growing by leaps and bounds so that millions of poor people are forced to live on the flood plain.'

**E** Comments made on the 2004 floods

# Taking a different look at the world

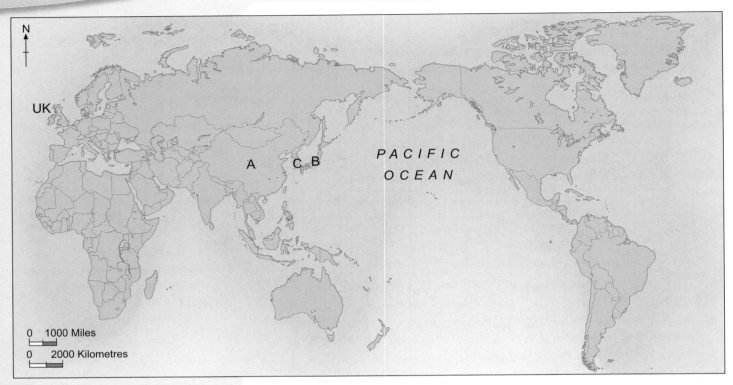

**A** World map

**B** Wealth of nations in 2000. This map does not show the real size of countries and world regions, but size according to total GDP (i.e. according to wealth).

**1** a) Look at the position of the UK on map **A**. How is this map different from most other maps of the world you have seen?
   b) Name the countries lettered A–C on map **A**.
   c) Which country matches each of these descriptions?
      (i) Population giant  (ii) Industrial giant of Asia
      (iii) Newly industrialising country and Asian Tiger

**2** a) Find the UK and Japan on map **B**. How is this map different from other maps you have seen?
   b) Are the UK and Japan more or less wealthy than indicated by their real sizes in map **A**?
   c) Describe what map **B** shows about the wealth of South and East Asia compared with sub-Saharan Africa.

**3** 'Around the sides of the Pacific Ocean are many of the world's most important countries.' Is this statement true or false? Explain your answer.

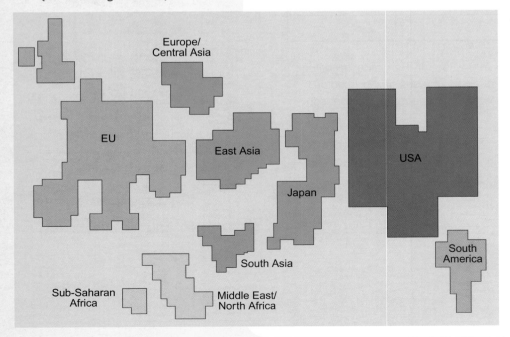

# SKILLS in geography

## 1 ATLAS SKILLS

### A How to use an atlas 1 – Countries of the world

1 Find the 'Contents' page in the front of your atlas.

2 Look for the heading 'World maps'.

3 Then search for a world 'political map'.

### B How to use an atlas 2 – Finding a place

1 Turn to the 'Index' at the back of your atlas.

2 Places are named in alphabetical order.

3 The page for the map you need is given first.

4 Its square is given second.

5 Next its latitude is stated, and then its longitude.

**Example:**

| Oxford, UK | 5 | 5E | 51° 46′N | 1° 15′W |
|---|---|---|---|---|
| | Page | Square | Latitude | Longitude |
| | | | 51 degrees | 1 degree |
| | | | 46 minutes | 15 minutes |
| | | | North | West |

**The amount of information given, and the order, varies from one atlas to another.**

## 2 OS MAP SKILLS

### A How to give a four-figure grid reference

1 Write down the number of the line that forms the left-hand side of the square – the easting – 31.

2 Write down the number of the line that forms the bottom of the square – the northing – 77 (see **A**).

3 Always write the numbers one after each other – do not add commas, hyphens, brackets or a space.

4 Write the number from along the bottom of the map first, then the number up the side – 3177.

### B How to give a six-figure grid reference

1 Write down the numbers of the line that forms the left-hand side of the square – the easting.

These are the same as the first two numbers in a four-figure grid reference – 31.

2 Imagine the square is then further divided up into tenths (see B). Write down the number of tenths the symbol lies along the line – 319.

3 Write down the number of the line that forms the bottom of the square – the northing. This is the same as the second two numbers in a four-figure grid reference – 77.

4 Imagine the side of the square is divided into tenths. Write down the number of tenths the symbol lies upwards in the square – 774.

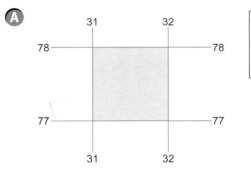

| |
|---|
| 1 – 31 |
| 2 – 77 |
| 3 and 4 – 3177 |

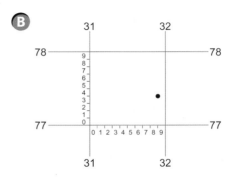

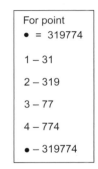

| For point |
|---|
| ● = 319774 |
| 1 – 31 |
| 2 – 319 |
| 3 – 77 |
| 4 – 774 |
| ● – 319774 |

## C How to draw a cross-section

When drawing a cross-section from an OS map, you will need to find out the height of the land. See the example below.

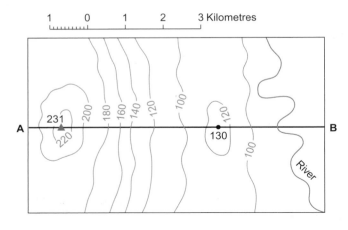

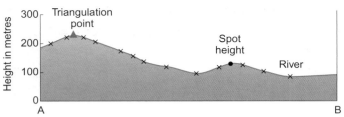

1 Place the straight edge of a piece of paper along the section and mark the start and end point of your section on the paper (AB).

2 Carefully mark on the paper the place where each contour line crosses. Note carefully the heights of the contour lines.

3 Mark on any interesting features, e.g. rivers, roads, spot heights.

4 Now draw a graph of your results. Draw a graph outline (see above). Note the lowest and highest contour height and use this to mark the vertical axis from 0 metres.

NB. Think carefully about the scale up the side – a good guide is 1 cm to 100 m for a 1:25 000 map.

5 Place your paper along the base of the graph and put small crosses on your graph at the correct heights and locations

6 Join the crosses together with a smooth curve – it is best to draw this freehand.

7 Add a title and labels for any key features, e.g. names of hills, rivers and roads.

# 3 GRAPHS THAT SHOW A TOTAL OF 100 PER CENT

This type of graph allows you to show the parts which make up a total. Think of using one of these four graph types whenever you have to present any data that has a total value of 100 (%). Graphs A–D all show the data in the table on the right.

| Vehicle type | Number |
|---|---|
| Buses | 20 |
| Cars | 70 |
| Lorries | 10 |
| Total | 100 |

**A ten-minute traffic count near the centre of a UK city**

1 Add up the values and make a total.

2 Draw a bar for the total value.

3 The bar can be either vertical or horizontal.

4 Add the scale to the sides of the bar.

5 Plot the different values.

## B Pictograph

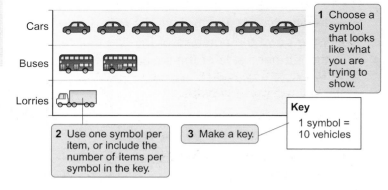

1 Choose a symbol that looks like what you are trying to show.

2 Use one symbol per item, or include the number of items per symbol in the key.

3 Make a key.

Key
1 symbol = 10 vehicles

## A Divided bar graph

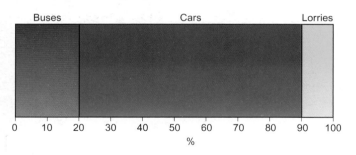

## C Pie graph

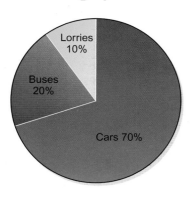

1 If you need to, turn the figures you are using into percentages.

2 Draw a circle.

3 Start at the top (12 o'clock) and draw the segments (from largest to smallest).

4 Make a key or label the segments.

## D Block graph

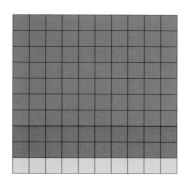

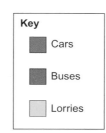

**Key**
- Cars
- Buses
- Lorries

1 Make a grid of 100 squares. Each square in the block shows 1 per cent.

2 Choose a different shade or colour for each value.

3 Shade or colour in the number of squares for the percentage.

4 Make a key.

# 4 OTHER GRAPHS

There are many different types of graphs. They are used all the time in geography. Sometimes it does not matter what type of graph you use. At other times, the type of data being shown needs a certain type of graph.

## A Line graph

Always use a line graph to show **continuous data**. For example, the only way to show temperature is in a line graph:

| J | F | M | A | M | J | J | A | S | O | N | D |
|---|---|---|---|---|---|---|---|---|---|---|---|
| 4 | 5 | 7 | 10 | 13 | 16 | 18 | 17 | 15 | 11 | 8 | 5 |

**Average monthly temperatures in London (°C)**

1 Draw the two axes, one vertical and one horizontal.

2 Label what each axis shows.

3 Look at the size of the values to be plotted.

4 Choose the scales and mark them on the axes.

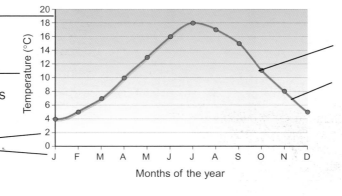

Months of the year

5 Plot the values by a dot or cross.

6 Join up the dots or crosses with a line.

## B Vertical bar graph

This graph is useful for showing data that changes every month, or every year. For example, the best way to show rainfall is as follows.

| J | F | M | A | M | J | J | A | S | O | N | D |
|---|---|---|---|---|---|---|---|---|---|---|---|
| 54 | 40 | 37 | 37 | 46 | 45 | 57 | 59 | 49 | 57 | 64 | 48 |

Average monthly rainfall in London (mm)

**1** Make a frame with two axes.

**2** Label what each axis shows.

**3** On the vertical axis make a scale, large enough for the highest number.

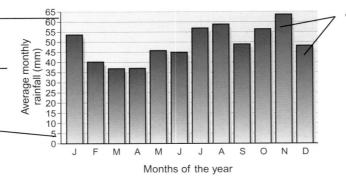

**4** From the horizontal axis draw bars of equal width.

## C Climate graph

### How to draw a climate graph

**1** Draw graph axes like those in the example here.

**2** Allow 12 cm on the horizontal axis for twelve months. Label these J, F, M, etc.

**3** Put a scale for rainfall on the lower part of the vertical axis.

**4** Above this put a scale for temperature.

**5** Plot the monthly rainfall figures as a bar graph.

**6** Plot the monthly temperature figures as a line graph. Place each cross or dot in the middle of the column because it is the average temperature for the month.

**7** Add a title and label the axes.

Climate graph for London, UK

### How to describe climate graphs

Climate graphs show a lot of data. So, where do you start? The guide below is to help you select the information that is most important. It will make it easier for you to compare the climates of two or more places.

Find the:

**1** highest temperature and month

**2** lowest temperature and month

**3** range of temperature (highest minus lowest)

**4** highest precipitation and month

**5** lowest precipitation and month

**6** precipitation distribution (all year, season with most).

These are the answers for the climate graphs shown.

**1** 18°C (highest temperature) in July (month)

**2** 4°C (lowest temperature) in January (month)

**3** 14°C (range of temperature)

**4** 64 mm (highest precipitation) in November (month)

**5** 37mm (lowest precipitation) in March and April (months)

**6** All year (there are no dry months)

## D Scatter graph

This type of graph is used to show the relationship between two sets of data.

| Year | Number of working age (15–64) for every person 65 years and older | Estimates for pension costs as a percentage of GDP |
|------|---|---|
| 2000 | 4.3 | 12.6 |
| 2010 | 3.8 | 13.2 |
| 2020 | 3.3 | 15.3 |
| 2030 | 2.8 | 20.3 |
| 2040 | 2.4 | 21.4 |

**1** Draw the two axes for the graph.

**2** Label the two axes.

**3** Choose suitable scales to cover the range of values.

**4** Place a cross or dot at the point where the two values meet.

**5** Do not join up the dots.

**6** If possible, draw a straight line which is the 'best fit' for all the points.

This graph shows a negative relationship (see below). As the number of people of working age **decreases**, pension costs **increase**.

If a relationship exists, it is possible to draw in the line of 'best fit' for all the points. The best fit line is always a straight line. It does not have to go through all the points. It is a summary line which shows the general relationship that exists between the two sets of values.

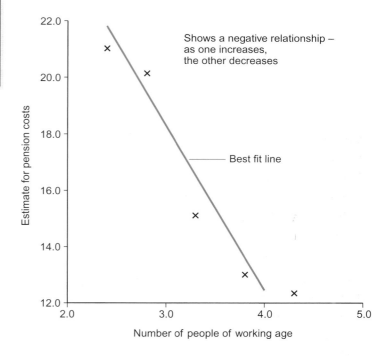

### What does the scatter graph show?
The three types of relationship are shows in graphs A–C below.

**A Positive relationship**
As the value of one increases, the value of the other increases as well. Both values increase at the same time.

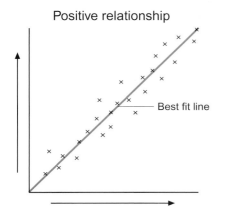

**B Negative relationship**
As the value of one increases, the value of the other decreases. One is increasing and the other is decreasing.

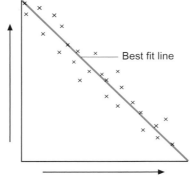

**C No relationship**
It is impossible to see a relationship. The values are scattered all over the place. Drawing a best fit line on the graph is impossible.

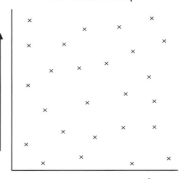

## E Population pyramid

1 Show the male population on the left and the female on the right.

2 Draw a horizontal axis with 0 in the middle. The scale can be in either percentages or numbers.

3 Draw a vertical axis from the 0. Divide into age groups, e.g. 0–4, 5–9, 10–14, etc.

4 Draw bars horizontally for each age group and gender.

5 Label the axes and add a title.

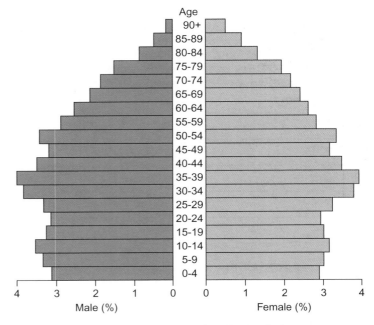

**Percentage male and female population**

## F Block bar graph

Block bar graphs are useful to show two or more values on the same graph. They can be vertical, as here, or horizontal.

1 Draw vertical and horizontal axes.

2 Draw bars for one set of values.

3 Above them draw bars for the second set of values, and so on.

4 Colour in each of the divisions and add a key.

5 Label the axes and add a title.

|  | Primary | Secondary | Tertiary |
|---|---|---|---|
| India | 65 | 30 | 5 |
| Japan | 8 | 30 | 62 |
| UK | 4 | 26 | 70 |

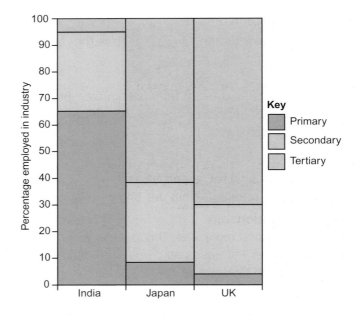

**Employment structure in various countries**

## G Living graph

1 Draw your graph outline and label the axes. Put the years or time along the bottom and the other value (e.g. *How Laura feels*) up the side.

2 Plot the graph to show how the value changes over time.

3 Add the labels in the correct places on the graph.

4 Add a title to your graph.

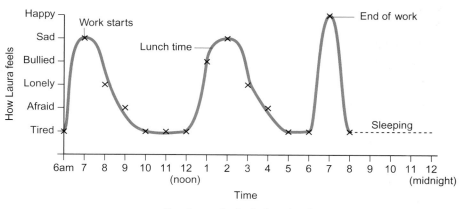

How Laura feels during the day

# 5 OTHER TYPES OF MAPS

## A How to draw a shading (choropleth) map

Shading (choropleth) maps show data for areas. If you have a table of data for named areas of the UK (or for anywhere else), it can be used to make a choropleth map.

1 Look at the highest and lowest values in your table of data, e.g. the highest and lowest wage.

2 Split the values up into four or five groups of equal size.

3 Choose a colour or type of shading for each group.

4 Very important – always choose darker colours for the data groups with the highest amounts (values).

5 Look at your data to see which areas on the map match each value group you set up in step 2. Shade or colour in each area correctly.

6 Remember to add a key!

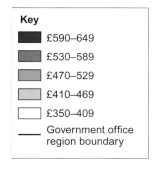

**Key**

| | |
|---|---|
| ▉ | £590–649 |
| ▨ | £530–589 |
| ▨ | £470–529 |
| ▨ | £410–469 |
| ☐ | £350–409 |
| ▬ | Government office region boundary |

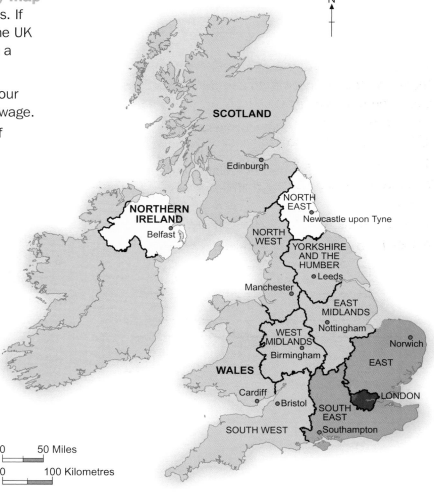

## B How to draw a flow map

1. Use a base map showing the places named.
2. Look at the size of the values and the space on your map.
3. Decide on a suitable scale for the width of the lines, e.g. 1 mm for each person or 2 mm for every 5 people, according to the space available.
4. Work out the different line widths.
5. Plot lines of varying width from areas A, B and C to the town.
6. Add a scale and a title to your map.

| Where people travelled from | Number of workers |
|---|---|
| Place A | 40 |
| Place B | 20 |
| Place C | 5 |

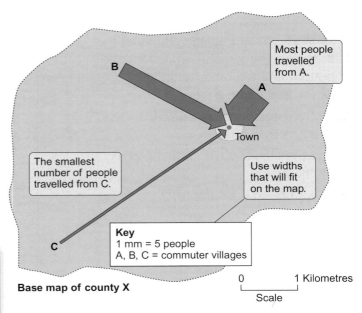

Base map of county X

## C How to measure distances on a map

Using the cross-section map and the instructions below, you can see that:

The distance between the spot height and the river along line A–B = 1 km

The distance between the trig point and the spot height along line A–B = 2.9 km

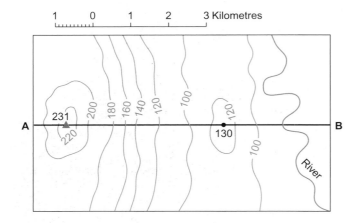

1. Using a piece of paper (or string if it is a winding distance) accurately mark the start and end point of the distance being measured.
2. Transfer the paper or string to the linear scale for the map.
3. Put the left-hand mark on the zero and accurately mark the total number of kilometres on the paper.
4. Measure the bit that is left using the divided section of the scale. This will be in metres.
5. Add the two together to give the final distance measured.
6. Remember to give the units (kilometres or metres) in your answer.

## D  How to draw a pictorial or mental map

Both use symbols, sketches and diagrams to show locations of geographical features on maps. Below is an example of a pictorial map to show farming. In a pictorial map, the map outline is always accurate and true. In a mental map, the map outline can be accurate, but it may also be distorted.

### Pictorial map

This shows what is actually located in an area.

1 Draw or trace accurately an outline map of the area.

2 Make up symbols, sketches, diagrams etc. which look like the features to be shown.

3 Put these in a key

4 Place them on the map where the features are located.

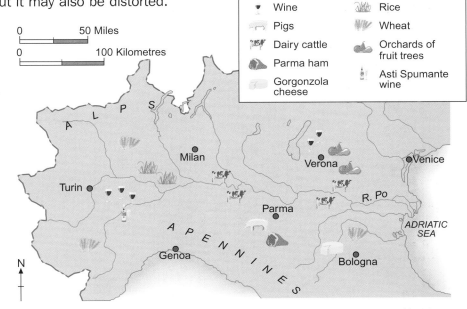

### Mental map

This shows what people think is located in an area; for geographical features actually located there, it shows what people think they look like.

1 Draw an outline map so that the area can be recognised, even if it is not totally accurate. Remote areas can be made to look further away than they really are.

2 Make up symbols, sketches, diagrams etc. which look like people imagine the features to be shown. Features can be made to look better or worse than they really are.

3 Put these in a key.

4 Place them on the map where people think the features are located.

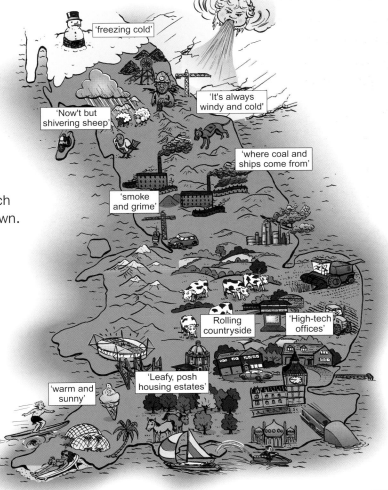

# SKETCHES

## How to draw a sketch map

The sketch map below was drawn to show differences in relief and drainage.

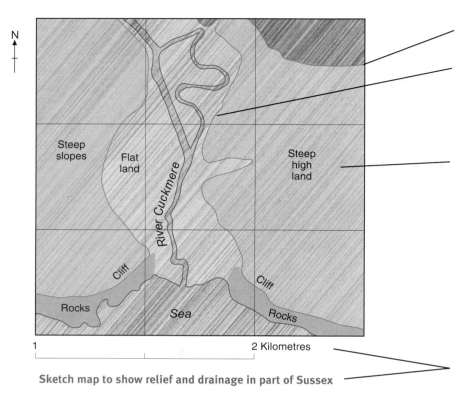

Steep slopes

Flat land

River Cuckmere

Steep high land

Cliff

Cliff

Rocks

Sea

Rocks

1          2 Kilometres

**Sketch map to show relief and drainage in part of Sussex**

**1** Draw a frame for your sketch map – think about its size and shape.

**2** In pencil, sketch the features you wish to show. Start with some accurate major features such as a coastline or road, or even lightly mark on the gridlines and numbers.

**3** Colour in your sketch map. Add a key for the symbols and colours you have used.

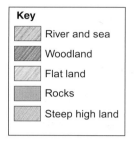

| Key | |
|---|---|
| | River and sea |
| | Woodland |
| | Flat land |
| | Rocks |
| | Steep high land |

**4** Add a title, north sign and scale.

## B  How to draw a labelled sketch from a photograph

**Cley next the Sea, Norfolk**

**1** Make a frame the same size as the photograph.

**2** In the frame, draw or trace the main features shown.

**3** Label the main physical and human features.

**4** Give your sketch a title.

Sunny weather

Windmill

Houses closely packed together

Trees

Village houses

Flat land covered by reeds

# 7 TIME COLUMNS

These are used to show what changes happened at key dates in the history of a place. The information contained helps with an understanding of its geography today.

## How to make a time column

1 Make a scale of dates down the side of the page.

2 Write in what happened at key dates.

3 Use } for a block of dates and write in what happened.

| Date | Information / changes | |
|------|----------------------|---|
| **1350** | Farming village | } Farming village |
| **1900** | Most houses around the sides of the village green | |
| **1901** | Mine opened; terraced houses built around the mine | } Mining settlement |
| **1906** | Railway station opened | |
| **1957** | Mine closed | |
| **1963** | Railway station closed | |
| **1971** | Motorway built nearby | |
| **1974** | Housing estates built | } Modern commuter settlement |
| **1994** | Becomes a commuter settlement | |

# 8 DIAGRAMS

## How to draw a spider diagram

1 Draw a circle (the 'body') in the middle of your page. Write the title in it, e.g. *Factors affecting farming*.

2 Draw lines ('legs') away from the circle.

3 Write an advantage at the end of each line, e.g. *Sunshine*, *Rainfall*, *Soil*.

4 You could draw a small sketch beside each advantage.

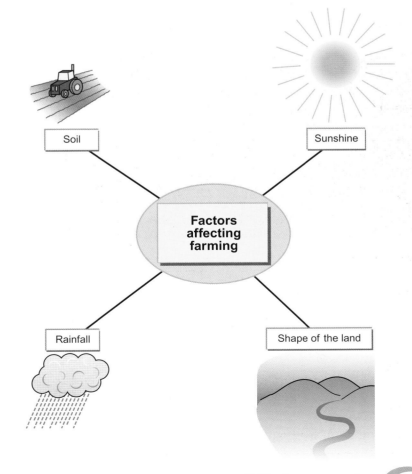

# Knowing your levels

## Key Stage 3 attainment targets

The targets set out below should help you measure your current level of attainment or realise what needs to be done to achieve your overall Key Stage 3 attainment target.

## Attainment descriptions

When looking at your own work or that of your classmates, try to use these bullet points to help you assess the work. Think about what you would need to do to get a piece of work to the next level.

To achieve **Level 2** you need to:

- Recognise physical features in the local area e.g. rivers, woods
- Recognise human features in the local area e.g. houses, shops, villages, roads
- Write about (describe) physical and human features in the local area
- Show an awareness of places outside of your local area
- Give your views about an environment or place
- Recognise how people affect the environment
- Select information from resources e.g. photographs, maps
- Use information from resources and what you have seen to answer and ask questions
- Use geographical words in your speaking and writing.

To achieve **Level 3** you also need to:

- Be able to compare the physical and human features of two different places – this means saying what is the same and what is different about places
- Give reasons (explain) for some of the features found in places
- Give your views about places and say why you have those views
- Talk or write about how people can improve places and maintain their quality for the future
- Answer a range of geographical questions using skills and resources
- Use a range of geographical vocabulary.

To achieve **Level 4** you also need to:

- Study a wider range of places and environments – at different scales and in different parts of the world
- Write about geographical patterns or distributions – be able to say where things are and where they are not
- Describe or write about physical processes e.g. river erosion and human processes e.g. migration
- Begin to understand how these processes can change a place and affect the people who live in an area
- Understand how people can improve or damage environments
- Give reasons for your own views and those of other people about a change to the environment
- Suggest geographical questions and investigate places/environments
- Collect primary and secondary data and present it in different ways and write about what it shows.

To achieve **Level 5** you also need to:

- Explain geographical patterns – why are some things found in some places but not in others?
- Explain the physical and human processes
- Describe how the processes lead to similarities and differences in environments and people's lives
- Recognise some links and relationships that make places and people dependent on others
- Suggest reasons for the ways human activity may change an environment and the different views people have
- Know what sustainable development is and how people try to achieve it
- Explain your own views about environments and places
- Begin to suggest geographical questions and issues
- Investigate places and environments using geographical skills and different ways of presenting information
- Select information, present it, write about it and draw sensible conclusions.

To achieve **Level 6** you also need to:

- Study places at a whole range of scales from local to global
- Describe and explain physical and human processes
- Recognise that processes interact to produce distinctive characteristics of places e.g. the climate in Europe is good for settlement and farming so many people live in this part of the world
- Describe how processes can interact and produce patterns and lead to changes in places e.g. over the last 50 years people have moved out of the centres of cities causing decline in inner cities – the pattern. This has led to a lot of redevelopment in inner cities and people are now moving back – changes.

- Appreciate the links and relationships that make places dependent on each other
- Recognise that there may be conflicting demands on an environment
- Describe and compare different approaches to managing environments
- Appreciate that people, including yourself, have different values and attitudes and that this results in different effects on people and places
- Carry out investigations to answer geographical questions and issues – collect primary and secondary data in different ways, present them using a range of skills, describe and explain what the data show and draw conclusions.

# Glossary

**Ageing population** Increasing percentage of old people (aged 65 and over) in a country.

**Air mass** A huge block of air, thousands of kilometres across, with the same temperature and moisture content.

**Air pressure** The 'weight' of the air pressing down on the Earth's surface.

**Altitude** The height in metres above sea level.

**Anticyclone** An area of high pressure where winds blow outwards.

**Aquifer** Underground store of water in permeable rock.

**Asylum-seeker** A refugee who applies to stay in another country because they face persecution and possibly death in their home country.

**Atmosphere** The 'envelope' of air masses that surrounds the Earth.

**Barometer** Instrument used to measure air pressure.

**Bauxite** A mineral from which aluminium is made.

**Birth rate** The number of births per 1000 people per year.

**Channel** Area between the banks where the river flows.

**Climate** An area's average weather over a period of time.

**Cloud** Millions of tiny water droplets or ice crystals.

**Colonies** Countries owned and governed by other countries.

**Communist or socialist** Countries where the State plans and runs most economic activities.

**Condensation** When water vapour, a gas, is changed into water as a liquid in water droplets and clouds by cooling.

**Consumer goods** Products made for people to buy.

**Convection current** When warm air rises through the air.

**Core region** Area most attractive for settlement and most densely populated in a region.

**Costs of production** Amount of money needed to make something.

**Death rate** The number of deaths per 1000 people per year.

**Depression** A swirling system with low pressure at the centre and fronts.

**Development** Level of growth and wealth of a country.

**Digital technology** Converting audio and video signals into a form that can be processed by computers and accurately reproduced (through the use of numbers, i.e. digits).

**Distribution** How the population of an area is spread.

**Drainage basin** Area of land drained by a river and its tributaries.

**Drought** Period of dry weather beyond that normally expected.

**Dynamic cities** Urban areas changing fast due to rapid economic growth.

**Economic migrant** Someone who moves to another country for a better standard of living.

**Eco-tourism** Allows tourists to have a good holiday but conserves the environment and involves the local people (also called green tourism).

**EU** The European Union, many countries in Europe have joined.

**Evaporation** When water from lakes and seas is changed into water vapour, a gas, by heating.

**Evapo-transpiration** Loss of water into the atmosphere from all surface sources.

**Fertility rate** Average number of children born to a woman in her lifetime.

**Floodplain** Area of flat land on the sides of a river.

**Fold mountains** Mountains formed by rocks being folded and uplifted.

**Front** The zone where two blocks of air meet.

**GDP (Gross domestic product)** The amount of money a country makes from the production of goods and services divided by the total population; the higher the GDP the richer the country.

**Gender** The sex of a person, male or female.

**Gorge** Deep, narrow, steep-sided valley.

**Groundwater flow** Movement of water through spaces and holes in rock.

**Heavy industries** Making large or bulky products such as ships and steel girders.

**Human attractions** Facilities for tourists built by people.

**Human development index (HDI)** A measure of the level of development calculated on the average income, life expectancy and literacy rate of a country's population.

**Infiltration** Downward movement of water into soil.

**Infrared** Radiation that is similar to light but invisible to humans; it can be used in photography.

**Interception** When rain is prevented from reaching the ground by trees.

**Isobar** A line on a weather map that joins together places with the same air pressure.

**Landscape** The natural scenery of an area and what it looks like.

**Lateral erosion** Wearing away the sides of the channel and valley.

**Latitude** The distances north or south of the Equator; lines of latitude are parallel to the Equator.

**Leakage** When much of the money paid for a holiday goes to companies based in richer countries instead of the country visited.

**LEDCs** Less Economically Developed Countries; the poorer countries of the world.

**Levees** Raised banks on the side of a river forming a natural embankment.

**Life expectancy** The average age to which people in a country are expected to live.

**Literacy rate** Percentage of adults who can read and write.

**Load** All materials transported by a river.

**Market** Place where goods are sold.

**Meander** Large bend in the river.

**MEDCs** More Economically Developed Countries; the richer countries of the world.

**Meteorologist** A person who studies the weather.

**Metropolitan** Built-up area around the main city.

**Migration** The movement of people.

**Millibars** Units used to measure air pressure.

**Monsoon** Climate with one season of heavy rainfall, as in India.

**Mouth** Point where a river goes into the sea.

**Natural decrease** When death rate is greater than birth rate.

**Natural hazard** Short-term event that is a danger to life and property.

**Natural increase** When birth rate is greater than death rate; birth rate minus death rate is the growth rate of the population.

**Natural resource** Something that occurs naturally that people can use.

**North Atlantic Drift** A warm ocean current.

**Onshore wind** When a wind blows from the sea to the land.

**Ox-bow lake** Semi-circular lake on the side of a river.

**Package holiday** An all-inclusive deal from a travel agent; the package usually includes travel, accommodation, food and some entertainment.

**Peninsula** An area of land surrounded on three sides by the sea.

**Periphery** Areas in a region that do not have very many people and do not favour settlement.

**Permeable rock** Rock with spaces and holes that allow water to pass through it.

**Physical attractions** Natural features that attract tourists, e.g. climate, rivers, mountains.

**Physical geography** The natural features on the Earth's surface.

**Population** The people who live in a place.

**Population density** The number of people per square kilometre.

**Population pyramid** A graph showing the population structure of an area, country or region.

**Population structure** The numbers of males and females in different age groups in a population.

**Precipitation** All forms of moisture that reach the ground surface, e.g. snow, rain, sleet, dew.

**Primary products** Raw materials from land and sea such as minerals and crops.

**Quality of life** How well someone can live, including health and education as well as wealth.

**Reclamation** Making land useful for settlement or farming.

**Refugee** A person who is forced to move to another country, usually as a result of civil war, persecution or a natural disaster.

**Region** Area of land with one or more similar features.

**Relief** The height and shape of the land.

**Reservoir** Artificial lake used to store water for human use.

**Runoff** Movement of water over the ground surface after precipitation.

**Satellite image** A photograph taken by a satellite camera high above the Earth's surface.

**Seasonal unemployment** When jobs are only available for part of the year, leaving people without work at other times.

**Secondary products** Products made from raw materials, such as chocolate bars made from cocoa beans.

**Service industry** Industry where people provide a service instead of making a product.

**Shanty town** Area of slums with hand-built shacks where the poorest people live.

**Silt** Fine-grained sediment carried and deposited by rivers.

**Soil erosion** Loss of fertile topsoil by wind and water.

**Source** Point where a river starts to flow.

**Standard of living** How well off and wealthy a person is.

**Staple crop** The most important food in people's diets.

**Subsistence** Living on what a family grows and produces for itself.

**Sustainable tourism** Tourism that does not damage the environment or the way of life of the local people.

**Terraced** Where level strips of land are cut out of hillsides.

**Tornado** A rapidly moving and vicious spiral of air that is smaller than a hurricane.

**Tourism** The industry that caters for visitors.

**Tourist** A person who travels away from home for a short time and intends to return home afterwards.

**Trade** The selling of goods between countries.

**Trade gap** The difference between the value of imports and exports in any country.

**Transpiration** Loss of water from plants to the atmosphere.

**Treaty** An agreement between different countries.

**Tributary** Smaller river that flows into a larger one.

**Tropical storm** Area of very low pressure with high winds and heavy rainfall.

**Vertical erosion** Wearing away land in a downward direction.

**Vicious cycle** Where one thing leads to another, which leads to another so that the situation gets worse and worse.

**V-shaped valley** River valley that is lowest in the centre.

**Water cycle** The movement of water between the air, the oceans and the ground.

**Water vapour** Water as a gas in the atmosphere.

**Waterfall** Where the river suddenly drops in height.

**Weather** The state of the atmosphere at any one time: whether it is sunny or raining, cloudy, hot, cold, etc.

**Weather forecast** A prediction of what the weather will be like.

**Weather station** A place used to record the weather with meteorological instruments.

**Western** Lifestyles in Europe and North America as opposed to those in the East, mainly Asia.

**Wind** Moving air from an area of high pressure to an area of low pressure.

# Index